Russia and the Politics of International Environmental Regimes

NEW HORIZONS IN ENVIRONMENTAL POLITICS

Series Editor: Arthur Mol, *Chair and Professor in Environmental Policy, Director, Wageningen School of Social Sciences, Wageningen University, The Netherlands, Professor in Environmental Policy, Renmin University, Beijing*

The New Horizons in Environmental Politics series provides a platform for in-depth critical assessments of how we understand the many changes in the politics of nature, the environment and natural resources that have occurred over the last 50 years. Books in the series question how the environment is (re)defined, debated and protected; explore differences between countries and regions in environmental politics; analyse how actors do and do not collaborate around environment and natural resource conflicts; describe who wins and who loses and in what ways; and detail how to better study, analyse and theorize such developments and outcomes.

The series is designed to promote innovative cross-disciplinary analysis of the contemporary issues and debates influencing the various dimensions of environmental politics. Covering a diverse range of topics, the series will examine the political, economic and ethical aspects of environmental policy, governance and regulation. It brings together cutting edge research on environmental politics worldwide in order to shed light on, and explain current trends and developments.

With oversight from the Series Editor, Professor Arthur Mol – a noted specialist in the field of environmental politics at Wageningen University, The Netherlands – the New Horizons in Environmental Politics series comprises carefully commissioned projects from experts in the field including both academics and professionals. The audience for the series is global, and books in the series are essential reading for students, academics and professionals – in short, anyone with an interest in understanding the vital issues affecting environmental politics in the twenty-first century.

Recent titles in the series include:

Subnational Partnerships for Sustainable Development
Transatlantic Cooperation between the United States and Germany
Holley Andrea Ralston

The Politics of Climate Change Negotiations
Strategies and Variables in Prolonged International Negotiations
Christian Downie

Russia and the Politics of International Environmental Regimes
Environmental Encounters or Foreign Policy?
Anna Korppoo, Nina Tynkkynen and Geir Hønneland

Russia and the Politics of International Environmental Regimes

Environmental Encounters or Foreign Policy?

Anna Korppoo

Senior Research Fellow, Fridtjof Nansen Institute, Norway

Nina Tynkkynen

Senior Research Fellow, University of Tampere, Finland

Geir Hønneland

Research Professor and Deputy Director, Fridtjof Nansen Institute, Norway

NEW HORIZONS IN ENVIRONMENTAL POLITICS

Cheltenham, UK • Northampton, MA, USA

Published by
Edward Elgar Publishing Limited
The Lypiatts
15 Lansdown Road
Cheltenham
Glos GL50 2JA
UK

Edward Elgar Publishing, Inc.
William Pratt House
9 Dewey Court
Northampton
Massachusetts 01060
USA

A catalogue record for this book
is available from the British Library

Library of Congress Control Number: 2014950756

This book is available electronically in the **Elgar**online
Economics Subject Collection
DOI 10.4337/9781782548645

ISBN 978 1 78254 863 8 (cased)
ISBN 978 1 78254 864 5 (eBook)

Typeset by Servis Filmsetting Ltd, Stockport, Cheshire
Printed and bound in Great Britain by T.J. International Ltd, Padstow

Contents

About the authors

Geir Hønneland has studied Russian fisheries management, and the Norwegian-Russian interface in the management of the Barents Sea fish resources, for nearly two decades. His work builds on participant observation in the Norwegian Coast Guard and the Joint Norwegian-Russian Fisheries Commission, as well as interviews with actors in the Russian fishing industry.

Anna Korppoo has been working on Russian climate change policies and politics at the international and domestic level since 2000. She has followed Russia's role in the international climate negotiations as an observer and and the implementation of the Kyoto mechanisms in transition economies. She has published several policy advice briefs as well as more academic works.

Nina Tynkkynen has studied Russian participation in international environmental politics, especially the politics of the Baltic Sea protection, since the early 2000s. She has published widely on Russian environmental policy and international environmental politics.

Preface

The international group of scholars studying Russia's engagement in international environmental politics is fairly small, perhaps because fieldwork in Russia entails challenges of its own. In any case, members of this group tend to know each other quite well. Anna Korppoo and Nina Tynkkynen have shared an involvement in these issues that date back to their Master's degree studies at the departments of Regional Studies and Environmental Policy as well as Slavonic Philology in the 'red' University of Tampere in Finland. When Anna relocated to the Fridtjof Nansen Institute in Norway in 2011, we recognized the interesting synergies with the research work of Geir Hønneland, who had lengthy experience of studying Russian environmental policy in the making, starting from his years as Russian-language interpreter for the Norwegian Coast Guard in the Barents Sea, back in the late 1980s and early 1990s. Putting together our knowledge of three issue areas of environmental policy that Russia had been negotiating at the international level seemed to form a comprehensive whole, as well as confirming our individual findings on how Russia looks at such processes.

It was Anna who took the practical initiative to this book project by arranging the first meeting in Oslo in June 2012. The process began smoothly: we found an interested publisher and worked on preparing our individual case studies. The writing process included several meetings in Oslo; we also organized a panel to discuss our topic at the Annual Conference of the British Association for Slavonic and East European Studies (BASEES) in Cambridge, UK, in the spring of 2013. The process, collaborating with scholars who have similar experiences of working in Russia and with the Russians, as well as the support that such a comparative approach to the cases gives to individual conclusions, has been a source of great inspiration and joy for all of us.

Anna has had main responsibility for Chapter 3 on climate politics, Nina for Chapter 4 on environmental protection in the Baltic Sea, and Geir for Chapter 5 on the Barents Sea fisheries management. Throughout the process, we have read and commented on each other's manuscripts and discussed them in order to facilitate detailed inter-case comparison. Chapters 1, 2, 6 and 7 have been written jointly by all three of us. We have aimed at standardizing the three case studies to some extent, while allowing some freedom for theme-specific needs. Russian-language words and text (mostly references) have been transliterated in line with the widely-used US Library of Congress system. Translations from Russian sources, mostly in the case-study chapters, are those of the authors themselves.

Many people have helped us during the writing process. First of all, we would like to mention our great colleague Jonathan Oldfield at the University of Birmingham, who kindly read through the book proposal as well as the entire manuscript of the book and offered useful comments. He also chaired our panel at the BASEES conference. We wish to express our gratitude to Jon for his support and professional – as well as more personal – inspiration during the process. Further, our warm thanks go to our language editor Susan Høivik and technical editor Maryanne Rygg, who once again worked tirelessly to improve the quality of our original text. Thank you also to commissioning editor Emily Mew and the production team at Edward Elgar for professional and swift management of the publication process. Further, our thanks go to our Russian colleagues and interviewees who have shared their expertise and views with us over the years, making a great contribution to our own knowledge bases.

This book fit in so well with our existing projects that several funders of our ongoing projects should be mentioned. Anna's work has been financed mainly by her post-doctoral research project 252853 of the Academy of Finland and her NORKLIMA (Climate Change and Impacts in Norway) project 207810 under the Research Council of Norway. Nina's work was funded by her Academy of Finland projects 131901 and 139686 as well as the Finnish Centre of Excellence in Russian Studies. Geir's work draws on several projects on Russian fisheries management, notably project 20110701 under the Research Council of Norway's HAVKYST (The Oceans and Coastal Areas) programme. Finally, the Fridtjof Nansen Institute has provided Anna and Geir with in-house funding for drafting the publication proposal as well as for finalizing the writing process.

As this project has stretched over a period of almost two years, it has overlapped with many important moments in our personal lives, some happy, some less so. Our final and most special thanks go to our spouses Juan Carlos, Veli-Pekka and Kristin and our families for all their support.

In Oslo and Tampere
Anna Korppoo, Nina Tynkkynen and Geir Hønneland

List of acronyms and abbreviations

Annex I	industrialized country group under the Climate Convention and the Kyoto Protocol
BSAP	Baltic Sea Action Plan of HELCOM, adopted in 2007
CBSS	Council of the Baltic Sea States
EEZ	exclusive economic zone
EBRD	European Bank for Reconstruction and Development
EU	European Union
GDP	gross domestic product
G77	developing country group in the UN climate negotiations
G8	the Group of Eight, eight leading industrialized countries
G20	the Group of Twenty, Finance Ministers and Central Bank Governors from 20 major economies
HELCOM	the Baltic Marine Environment Protection Commission, also known as the Helsinki Commission
ICES	International Council for the Exploration of the Sea
IMO	International Maritime Organization
IPCC	Intergovernmental Panel on Climate Change
IR	international relations
JI	joint implementation
JPC	Joint Comprehensive Environmental Action Programme, launched by HELCOM in 1992
NATO	North Atlantic Treaty Organization
NDEP	Northern Dimension Environmental Partnership
NECA	NOx Emission Control Area
Nefco	Nordic Environment Finance Corporation
NGO	non-governmental organization
NIB	Nordic Investment Bank
OECD	Organisation for Economic Co-operation and Development
PINRO	Knipovich Polar Research Institute of Marine Fisheries and Oceanography
PPP	public-private partnership
PSSA	Particularly Sensitive Sea Area (PSSA)
RAO UES	Russia's electricity monopoly RAO 'Unified Energy System' of Russia, dismantled in 2008

TAC	total allowable catch
UN	United Nations
US	United States
USSR	The Union of Soviet Socialist Republics, dissolved in 1991
VNIRO	Russian Federal Research Institute of Marine Fisheries and Oceanography
WTO	World Trade Organization
WWF	Worldwide Fund for Nature

1. Introduction

RUSSIA IN THE GLOBAL ENVIRONMENT

Russia's environment is of global importance, for many reasons. First, as the largest country on Earth, Russia remains a major contributor to regional and global environmental degradation. It is the fourth largest emitter of greenhouse gases in the world and a major supplier of fossil fuels – the main single source of greenhouse gases on a global scale. Transboundary air and water pollution originating from Russia gives rise to concern, especially in the neighbouring countries.

The main reason for industrial pollution and the high energy intensity of the Russian economy lies in the deteriorating and inadequately maintained infrastructure built during the Soviet era. Air pollution is deemed high or extremely high in about half of the federal subjects (regions), according to the Russian Ministry of Natural Resources and Environment (Ministerstvo 2010). The number of people living in such areas is about 54 million. Moreover, together with the legacy of Soviet economic planning and the authoritarian system of governance, the country's economic and societal transition has obstructed the development of environmental policy and management (Henry and Douhovnikoff 2008, p.437). This gives rise to fundamental questions about Russia's ability to limit the negative impacts on the environment through domestic efforts alone. At the same time, the situation works as an incentive for Western investment in Russia's environmental sector, creating *win–win* opportunities for both parties.

Second, Russia's natural resources are among the most abundant in the world: for example, Russia accounted for 20 per cent of the total global forest area as of 2010 (FAO 2010, p.12) and 21.4 per cent of proven natural gas resources in 2011 (BP 2012, p.10). According to a recent WWF report, Russia's natural environment is capable of compensating for a footprint of more than six hectares per person – this is considered to make the country a *donor* to the global environment, as its own environmental footprint is nearly one-third less (*Ria Novosti*, 15 May 2012). Russia is also one of the world's leading fishing nations, ranking fifth in 2010 in terms of volume in capture fisheries (FAO 2012). However, serious depletion threatens these resources. According to expert estimates, without a sustainable forest management policy, Russian forests are likely to turn from net absorbers of carbon dioxide to net emitters by 2040, because of forest fires, the increasing age of the forests, the spread of tree pests and diseases, and harmful logging practices.[1] Also significant associated petroleum gas reserves have been lost by flaring them as a waste side-product. The 2009 legislation introduced restrictions on this practice, but implementation has been slow (see Kiryushin et al. 2013).

All in all, then, today's Russia has a significant role to play in global environmental and natural resource politics. This also motivates other countries and international actors, the EU in particular, to engage Russia in global environmental politics and to encourage it to take commitments that can facilitate the development of domestic environmental policy. The Russian Federation is a signatory to almost all major international environmental and natural resource agreements, and it participates, albeit not always very actively, in all main environmental policy processes underway at the global level (see Oldfield, et al. 2003; Jørgensen and Hønneland 2006). In addition, especially in the latter half of the 1980s and throughout the 1990s, Russia has been the focus of transnational efforts to promote environmental protection in the country.

Participation in global environmental processes is seldom motivated by environmental considerations alone (see Barkdull and Harris 2002). Nor are agreements exclusively about the environment: they also involve international relations, geopolitics, resource struggles, scientific debates, trade issues, domestic policy struggles, and the like. In his analysis of East–West environmental politics from the 1960s to the 1990s, Robert Darst (2001) notes that both sides often used environmental cooperation to create an image of cooperativeness and to facilitate collaboration in non-environmental issues as well. For example, it is widely accepted that, when the Soviet Union played a leading role in establishing the Long-Range Transboundary Air Pollution regime in the late 1970s, it was motivated largely by the desire to stand out as cooperative and pro-active in international environmental politics in general (see also Hønneland and Jørgensen 2003). Regardless of the concessions required, also the ratification of the Kyoto Protocol was seen by the Russian side as an image-building exercise; this ratification is still often referred to as 'a political decision' (see Korppoo et al. 2006, p. 23). The foreign policy and diplomacy traditions of participating states inevitably define their mode of negotiation in international environmental politics. Moreover, as suggested by the metaphor of a two-level game (see below), international and domestic policy goals mutually constitute the state's position *vis-à-vis* the international regime. Accordingly, state involvement in international environmental regimes is not simply a matter of strictly environmental concerns.

This is precisely where we put the spotlight in this book: what is involved in Russia's interfaces with other states within the framework of international environmental politics today? Our working hypothesis is that these are not merely '*environmental* encounters', but reflections of more general foreign and domestic policies on the part of Russia, and are sometimes also seen as useful 'platforms' for image-building and benefit-seeking, and not primarily the promotion of specific environmental goals.

AIM OF THE STUDY

In this book we analyse Russia's participation in international environmental regimes[2] by delving into Russian discourses concerning the issues raised by such regimes, and how regime provisions are adopted at the domestic level. We ask:

- What kinds of policy issues arise in the interfaces between international relations and Russian domestic politics in these specific fields?
- What are the motivations behind Russian policy positions?
- How well do Russia's international negotiation positions correspond with its domestic discourses?

We examine examples of international environmental cooperation in three highly topical fields: *climate policy, water protection* and *fisheries management*.

This choice of cases may provide stronger evidence of repeating patterns between environmental fields than, for instance, focusing solely on UN-level negotiations, because it may reveal practices that are more deeply rooted than for instance diplomatic training or strategic planning in Russia's various governance bodies. As fields of environmental cooperation, these three cases represent different kinds of cases in terms of coverage. Whereas the climate change regime is negotiated multilaterally under the global umbrella of the UN, the water protection case presented here comes from regional cooperation among the countries with access to the Baltic Sea, and the fisheries management case is an example of bilateral negotiations between Russia and Norway.

Russia has participated in global climate policy-making since the field was recognized as globally important in the late 1980s. Soviet scientists were actually among the first to discuss the phenomenon as a problem,[3] but the Western governments were able to dedicate more money for research after the collapse of the Soviet Union. Under the climate convention, the newly established Russia had to take a more marginal role at first, and was granted significant concessions (surplus allowances) as a reaction to the negative effects of the economic transition very much supported by the West. Russia turned from a bystander into an active market promoter after the Kyoto Protocol introduced the Kyoto flexible mechanisms, which opened the possibility of Russia selling its surplus emitting allowances to other governments. But the US withdrawal from the Kyoto pact led to a dramatic decline in demand, disappointing many Russian stakeholders.

Cooperation on the protection of the Baltic Sea environment started back in the early 1970s, and the 1974 Helsinki Convention on the protection of the marine environment of the Baltic Sea area was joined also by the Soviet Union. Encompassing all the coastal states of the sea, the regime has since then issued policy recommendations on environmental protection and guided various scientific activities. Primarily, however, the regime has served as a diplomatic venue between 'East' and 'West', as the Baltic Sea lies on the Cold War dividing line between these two.

And, turning to the third main field of study here, the Barents Sea fisheries management regime was established in the mid-1970s between Norway and the Soviet Union, as a result of major changes in the law of the sea at the time. Coastal states were given the right to manage fisheries in economic zones up to 200 nautical miles from the shore. The two countries immediately agreed to split the major fish stocks in the Barents Sea – including the world's largest cod stock. This cooperation has later been expanded to include coordination in a wide range of fisheries management tasks, including enforcement and technical regulations like mesh size.

We analyse storylines and discourses that characterize Russian participation in the three international environmental regimes, as well as in politics at the domestic level. We have chosen discourse analysis because it takes the explanation beyond mere reference to interests, and allows a focus on how interests unfold in the context of specific socio-historical discourses and institutional practices. It also provides conceptual tools for analysing controversies in their wider political context. Thus, the focus on discourses helps to bring out the motivations behind policy positions. By examining domestic discourse we may learn more about the internal *hinterland* that foreign policy decision-makers *might* take into account. If domestic discourse on a topic within international environmental politics centres on non-environmental factors (for example, economic benefits rather than emissions reductions), *and* that is also the case with Russia's stance in the international regime, then we might plausibly expect a link between domestic discourse and international practice. Our study thus provides flesh to the bones of the discussion on why Russia acts as it does in international environmental politics.

In explaining why Russia acts as it does we lean on the literature on the intersection of comparative politics and international relations (IR) which emphasizes the interactive relationship between domestic and foreign policies in explaining a state's approach to international policy-making (see Rosenau 1969; Krasner 1978; Putnam 1988). This relationship is bound to shift over time, so the relative weights of international and domestic factors will vary. The metaphor of a two-level game, introduced by Robert Putnam, sees the politics of international policy-making as a game in which domestic groups pursue their interests by pressuring the government to adopt favourable policies, while governments seek to satisfy these pressures and simultaneously minimize the adverse consequences of developments abroad (Putnam 1988, p. 434). The metaphor thus suggests that domestic and international goals are often entangled, forming 'synergistic issue linkages', and that international and domestic politics are mutually constitutive of each other.

Laura Henry and Lisa McIntosh Sundstrom (2012, p. 1317) argue that in contexts like that of Russia, where meaningfully democratic political institutions are lacking, approaches to international policy-making are more influenced by the executive leader's framing of national interest than by tough domestic bargaining. As Putnam's model entails analysing the bargaining processes in detail, we do not apply it as such here; however, in the discussion part of this book, we use the metaphor to reflect the discourses identified in the cases *vis-à-vis* the wider agendas of the domestic and foreign policy levels. This is to show how the motivations behind Russia's conduct in international environmental regimes are based on the larger agendas of these policy levels, rather than on environmental concern as such.

The overarching goal of our analysis is to contribute to the understanding of Russia's conduct in international environmental regimes. This is important not only because of the specific importance of Russia as regards global ecological systems, but also because of the acknowledged need to complement international environmental policy analysis by studies that are sensitive to diverse systems of environmental management and governance across the post-socialist region (see Oldfield 2005, p. 16). Our study is intended contribute to the understanding of the dynamics of Russia's environmental policy-making at large: not only will it tell something about changes that international environmental regimes trigger in Russia and the limitations set by various domestic economic and political dynamics – it can also help other parties to see more deeply behind the Russian position, which may at times seem obscure. In turn, this should facilitate interpreting Russian positions in future negotiations.

METHODOLOGY: ENVIRONMENTAL DISCOURSE

Our research material builds on the study of public documents, numerous interviews and (partly participant) observation. The empirical material is explained in detail in the case studies; the empirical information and insights presented here are based on the authors' 15-plus years of experience in the subject matter; and specific material for the case studies has come from various research projects in which the authors have been involved over the years. It is against this backdrop that we map Russian discourses and practices regarding its involvement in international environmental regimes.

Although the term 'discourse' is employed in widely varying ways in the social sciences, the modern concept of *discourse analysis* generally refers to a type of research activity carried out from a post-modernist viewpoint, aimed at revealing the influence of language on human behaviour and society. Along with other theories in the post-positivist tradition, discourse analysis aims at explaining how actors' interests are formed, whereas theories in the realist and institutionalist traditions take actors' interests largely for granted (see, for example, Jørgensen 2010).

What, then, is a *discourse* – a word that in everyday speech is used to refer to a discussion or a conversation?[4] In his textbook on discourse analysis, Neumann (2001, p.17) lists various definitions of the term, ranging from '*a process* reflecting a distribution of knowledge, authority, and social relationships, which propels those enrolled in it' (see Barth 1993), and '*a system* for the formation of statements' (see Bartelson 1995), to '*practices* that systematically form the objects of which they speak' (see Foucault 1972) (emphasis added). We may add to this list definitions that present a discourse as '*a shared way of apprehending the world*' (Dryzek 1997, p.8, emphasis added) and '*a specific ensemble of ideas, concepts, and categorizations* that are produced, reproduced, and transformed in a particular set of practices and through which meaning is given to physical and social realities' (Hajer 1995, p.44, emphasis added). However, more important than this sizeable divergence in categorizing discourse as a source or reflection of something is the conception of what this 'something' contains and what its effects are. Discourses are generally seen as producing or reflecting specific ideas, concepts or statements. These, in turn, are held to affect those who produce (or reflect) them or their context. Hence, discourse is 'something' that affects the way 'someone' conceives of and talks about 'something'. The challenge lies in identifying that social 'something' which brings forth, affirms and preserves specific modes of understanding, and revealing *how our understanding of the world is created, maintained and reproduced.*

We draw on the approach to environmental discourse offered by Hajer (1995). According to Hajer, actors can make sense of the world only by drawing on the terms of the discourses available to them. Hence, persons are *constituted* by discursive practices. Hajer further contends that change and permanence alike are caused by social practices, ascribing both to 'active discursive reproduction or transformation' (1995, p. 56). He takes up Davies and Harré's (1990) concept of *storylines* as a main mechanism in this respect, defining the concept as 'a generative sort of narrative that allows actors to draw upon various discursive categories to give meaning to specific physical or social phenomena' (Hajer 1995, p. 56). A storyline captures certain aspects of a problem complex in a simple and understandable manner. The argument is that people draw on such simplified representations of 'reality' rather than complex systems of knowledge in creating a cognitive comprehension of a subject matter. Storylines play a key role in positioning subjects in a discourse. They re-order people's understandings of problems and can thereby cause political change. Therefore, finding the appropriate storyline becomes an important mechanism of political agency. Once a storyline has been established in a discourse, it settles in as 'the way we talk around here'. Even when the objective is to challenge a dominant storyline, people can be expected to position themselves in terms of known categories, expressing themselves within the same discursive frame. And so, society is reproduced in a process of interaction between active agents and constraining structures – a process that constantly re-invents the social order.

In line with the example given by Hajer, we approach the discourses through storylines in order to distinguish the orientations of different actors in different domestic discussions on Russia's participation in international environmental regimes. This methodology enables us to analyse how various interests are constituted and play out in the context of specific socio-historical discourses. It also provides conceptual tools for analysing controversies over various issues in their wider political context. Thus, the focus on discourses helps to indicate the motivations behind policy positions, and to recognize also the 'non-environmental' side of the story.

STRUCTURE OF THIS VOLUME

In Chapter 2, we begin by situating our approach within the wider context of international environmental politics, followed by an overview of major trends in international environmental politics of recent decades. Then we introduce the Russian system of environmental governance, and examine its evolution since the Russian Federation was established as the successor-state to the Soviet Union in 1992. In addition to the environmental bureaucracy, there are various other powerful institutional structures and actors that are pivotal in determining Russia's conduct in international environmental regimes. We also provide a brief introduction to Russian foreign policy, pointing out how certain cleavages have dominated the Russian foreign policy debate for nearly two centuries, and outlining the basic approaches that define Russia's external relations in the environmental sector as well.

The two introductory chapters are followed by three chapters focusing on the three case studies outlined above: on climate politics, on water protection and on fisheries management. Each of these chapters starts by outlining the problem at hand and the international regime that has been established to handle it. Then we go on to map the general Russian discourse surrounding the issue, before presenting the Russian stance taken in the international regime. We also provide a description of how the issue is dealt with in domestic Russian politics, in order to situate the national discourse and Russian international-level practice in a broader context. On that basis, in Chapter 6 we discuss the extent to which Russia's participation in the international regimes is indeed a reflection of *environmental* encounters with other states – or whether it is more an expression of broader Russian foreign and domestic policy concerns, and what kind of concerns. This question is debated on a broader scale in the concluding chapter.

NOTES

1. See Angelina Davydova (2013), 'Russia's silence on climate change helps no one', The Conversation, 25 November, available at: http://theconversation.com/russias-silence-on-climate-change-helps-no-one-20661 (accessed 31 March 2014).
2. The terms 'agreement', 'arrangement' and 'regime' are used interchangeably in this book. For all practical purposes, we will be dealing with one specific international agreement, or more commonly a set of interrelated agreements, and the related institutional setting, such as conferences, panels, commissions and secretariats.
3. Soviet scientists were very active in authoring the first key reports of the Intergovernmental Panel on Climate Change (1990, 1992). See also Budyko and Izrael (1987).
4. This and the following discussion draw on Hønneland (2003).

2. Environmental regimes and Russia's approaches to environmental and foreign policy

THE CONTEXT: INTERNATIONAL ENVIRONMENTAL REGIMES

International environmental problems have been on the political agenda for some four decades now.[1] International agreements are the means through which lofty ambitions are intended to translate into practical measures and outcomes in specific areas. It is easy enough for governments to profess allegiance to forward-thinking policies at international conferences, because such statements are not binding. The traditional approach to dealing with that problem has been to establish multilateral environmental agreements. The number of international treaties in existence depends on how you count them, but they certainly number in the hundreds, and many of them have appeared in the course of the last 20 to 30 years. The great majority of treaties are bilateral. There is a sizeable number of regional treaties as well, but far fewer global ones – because environmental problems can usually be dealt with more effectively at lower levels. Nevertheless, it is the global treaties that generally attract most attention among policy-makers and the media. This is because they concern the environmental problems that are the most difficult to solve and that, as a result, lead to heated political and economic debates linked to responsibilities and equity between nations.

Although a few scattered conservation agreements had appeared in the early years of the twentieth century, the 1972 Stockholm Conference on the Human Environment is generally considered the watershed event that sparked a genuinely international approach to the environment. The conference resulted in several international agreements in the field of 'classic' nature conservation – the protection of endangered species, for example. As the 1970s progressed, treaties targeted air and water pollution, usually within a demarcated part of the globe. By the 1980s, pollution had become a worldwide concern, and initiatives now tended to promote global-level responses to reduce emissions of substances known to deplete the ozone layer. In 1987, the UN released the report of the Brundtland Commission *Our Common Future: Towards Sustainable Development*, which launched the concept of 'sustainable development' – defined as 'development that meets the needs of the present without compromising the ability of future generations to meet their own needs' (World Commission on Environment and Development 1987). The UN Convention on the Law of the Sea, negotiated since 1973 and concluded in 1982, was followed by another pivotal event, the 1992 Conference on Environment and Development held in Rio de Janeiro. That summit resulted in several important agreements, including conventions on biological diversity and climate change. Perhaps most importantly, the precautionary principle – stipulating the need to take policy action to prevent serious future environmental risks regardless of current scientific uncertainty[2] – was established as a leading principle in international environmental politics.

International environmental agreements have become increasingly ambitious and sophisticated. The first treaties, back in the 1970s, did little more than acknowledge the existence of a certain problem and list ambitious plans, without setting targets or prescribing specific courses of action. The most important accomplishment of these agreements was to alert the political establishment to the problem, spurring systematic efforts to learn more about it. During the 1980s, there emerged a new generation of agreements that set numerical targets and deadlines for emission cuts. The 1987 Montreal Protocol, a key document of the ozone regime, was one of the first agreements to adopt this approach, which quickly found its way into other agreements on air and sea pollution. Targets were often rather randomly set, but these agreements nevertheless represented a significant advance over the first generation, not least because progress (or lack of it) could now be measured. The cost-effectiveness of implementation and considerations of equity between industrialized and developing countries became norms. Nature's capacity to absorb or tolerate harm was also taken into consideration.

The emergence of complex environmental problems that penetrate the key functions of societies like energy and technology, such as climate change and ozone-layer depletion, has brought environmental negotiations closer to the everyday lives of industrial actors as well as consumers. The expenses and societal changes expected because of international commitments have led governments, concerned about their popularity ratings, to opt for 'foot-dragging' strategies or directly obstruct progress – as in the case of the climate negotiations. Further, some have questioned the suitability of the UN as the forum for multilateral negotiation, due to its consensus-based decision-making system which is prone to interruptions orchestrated by various vested interests as well as unilateral withdrawals of major polluters (in many cases, this has been the US). Achieving consensus on what should be done, who should do it, who should pay and who has a right to take such decisions, has proven very difficult at the global level. Given the deadlock in climate negotiations preceding the 2009 Copenhagen summit, some experts have even opined that the era of UN-based legally binding environmental regimes is coming to an end, and predict that future regimes will be based on voluntary approaches instead (Kuik et al. 2008; Gupta 2006). Other forums for environmental cooperation beyond the UN have been explored; and climate change in particular has featured on the agenda of more exclusive high-level international political forums like G-8 and G-20 – with little success as yet.

International environmental agreements that commit national governments to binding targets must be translated into national level policies, in order for the country to comply with the commitments entailed by the agreement. Such legal commitment is confirmed by ratification of an international agreement. As a rule, this is followed by more detailed national legislation intended to regulate which domestic actors should reduce their environmental impact and to what extent. Governments can choose among various policy instruments to identify those that best fit their national conditions, so national environmental governance systems emerge with individual characteristics. Policy-makers have the classic choice between regulatory and market-based policy instruments – the former being the more conventional and less flexible 'command-and-control' option, whereas the latter allow market signals to direct the choice of implementation (see, for example, Stavins 2000). Occasionally, set targets are achieved as a side effect of a policy that actually targeted a different goal: here the impact of economic downturns on greenhouse gas emissions is a clear practical example.

INTERPRETATIONS OF SUSTAINABLE DEVELOPMENT IN RUSSIA

Scientific circles in Russia have questioned the Russian translation of the concept *ustoichivoe razvitie*, which relates more to the idea of 'stable development' (for an English language overview of the conceptual debate, see Oldfield and Shaw 2002; Oldfield 2001), and thus fails to capture the essence of development that is *sustainable* and not merely 'stable'. In that understanding, Russia's relatively advanced scientific and technical capabilities are seen as a basis for the successful implementation of sustainable development, at home and abroad (Oldfield 2005, p. 72). Overall, Russian interpretations of 'sustainable development' are in line with the recent trend in the country's environmental policy, of emphasizing natural resource *management* rather than environmental *regulation* (Tynkkynen 2010). The idea of sustainable development is reflected in key environmental legislation and associated policy initiatives established in Russia since the early 1990s,[3] indicating a 'general concern for improving the efficiency of natural resource use and reducing the pollution-intensity of the country's industrial system with efforts to connect such ecologising intentions to wider social issues' (Oldfield 2005, p. 75). In April 2012, a document titled 'Principles of the state policy in the area of environmental development of the Russian Federation for the period up to the year 2030' was introduced. While outlining a range of social and economic principles in the sphere of environmental policy, it presents no practical policy instruments – for which it has been criticized by environmental non-governmental organizations (NGOs) (see *St Petersburg Times*, 2 May 2012). Regardless, civil servants interviewed by the authors of this book say that such broad policy documents can be useful, as they provide a mandate for acting.

A key aspect of sustainable development and the associated environmental policy is the importance of Russia for the state of the global environment (Oldfield 2005, p. 72). This view stresses the country's vast natural resources and ecological reserves, and is allied to the argument that Russia should be compensated for its ecological services – for example, for its forests acting as a 'carbon sink' (see Kontratev et al. 2003, pp. 12–13; Tynkkynen 2010; UNDP 2010). Notably, several attempts to restore the nation's great power status have relied on Russia's natural resources. As Anikin (2002, p. 314, translated by Nina Tynkkynen) notes: 'despite all the disturbances in recent years, Russia remains a great power because its potential of natural resources is about two times the potential of the USA, about five to six times that of Germany, and about 18 to 20 times that of Japan. This is one part of our idea of Great Russia.' Geographer N.N. Klyuev from the Geographical Institute at the Russian Academy of Sciences introduced the idea of Russia as a 'great ecological power' [*ekologicheskaya derzhava*] in an article published in 2002: 'The Russian Federation is the leading ecological power, whose environment determines the ecological future of our planet', he writes (2002, p. 5). Given the numerous environmental 'hot spots' located in Russian territory, all this may sound rather questionable to a Western observer. Russia's natural resources-driven understanding of the environment does not match the environmental protection-based starting point taken by the West. Western environmental policy focuses on regulating the damage that human activity does to the state of the environment (quality), whereas the Russian approach emphasizes the economic opportunities retrievable from the environment (quantity), and links damage to the environment to harm done to human health.

No doubt, Russia's general modernization agenda has advanced (or may advance) certain elements of ecological modernization too, especially as regards the improvement of energy efficiency and attempts to diversify the economy. For example, the report *Projection of Long-term Social and Economic Development of the Russian Federation until 2030*, approved by the prime minister in 2013, for the first time provided official data on the projected peaking of greenhouse gas (GHG) emissions beyond 2020, declining back to 70 per cent of the reference level by 2030.[4] According to this projection, achieving these targets will require improved energy efficiency and the introduction of energy-saving technologies. However, it should be noted here that even though the economic transition from state socialism to market democracy during the 1990s was expected to bring ecological improvement – and some improvement in the ecological situation did result – modernization did not lead to improved environmental institutions, but to ecological subversion (see Andersen 2002) or environmental deinstitutionalization (Mol 2009). Consequently, the linkage between modernization in general and ecological modernization should not be overemphasized.

ACTORS IN RUSSIAN ENVIRONMENTAL POLICY

There is a highly diverse range of actors relevant for environmental policy and governance in Russia. First of all come state actors like the government and the various administrative bodies. On top of the environmental administration (see below), other administrative branches significantly influence environmental policy-making, especially those related to economy, energy, housing, transport and industry. The president has a greater role in environmental policy-making than in many European democracies; during the Medvedev presidency, many important reforms were pushed forward by the activity of the president. Medvedev regularly took up environmental aspects and in his speeches called for consolidation of environmental policy,[5] which was seen as a mandate to act at lower levels of administration. President Putin, however, seems less willing and able to improve his environmental record seriously. However, he also occasionally emphasizes environmental aspects, at least at the rhetorical level (see Henry and McIntosh Sundstrom 2012, pp. 1301–2).

Private enterprises and business associations are an important actor group for environmental policy-making and ecological modernization in Russia. Most significantly, this concerns industrial and energy sector actors. These industries form an influential lobby and have managed to affect state environmental policies in ways that best suit their businesses. Their position has been strongly supported by the government policy of emphasizing economic growth based on the extraction of natural resources. Kotilainen et al. (2008, p.72) note that in some industrial sectors, forest industry in particular, 'a partial shift in emphasis during the post-Soviet period from the regulation of environmental issues by the state towards governance by enterprises, on the one hand, and non-governmental organisations, on the other, can be identified'. One example of their influence on environmental policy-making is the case of the Sakhalin oil and gas project: the Russian Ministry for Natural Resources accused the foreign investors of infringing environmental laws so as to be able to get the project transferred from foreign companies to Russia's Gazprom (Tokunaga 2010, p.1700).

In the Soviet Union, the scientific community was needed to counsel and support projects undertaken by the government to create energy, extract raw material, or utilize natural resources (see, for example, Ostergren and Jacques 2002). In contemporary Russia, the scientific community has been replaced by the participation of various interest groups including business elites, especially those involved in extractive industry. The role of the scientific community in environmental policy-making has weakened also because state funding of scientific work has been cut drastically. Accordingly, Russia is now suffering from a lack of environmental experts: there are not enough ecologists or other specialists who can understand issues related to ecology and development at large (see Yanitsky 2007).

Even though public opinion polls consistently show high levels of environmental concern among members of the public, the current level of environmental activism is relatively low in Russia (see Henry and Douhovnikoff 2008). Today's environmental movement is versatile: environmental NGOs range from local to national and transnational groups working on diverse topics such as environmental education and recreation, air and water pollution, or nuclear waste (Tynkkynen 2006; Henry 2010). Changing domestic political and economic conditions have not had much effect on the limited political weight of the organizations – at least, not any positive effect.

Finally, international actors are influential for Russia's policy-making. In the 1990s, Russia committed itself to more than 30 bilateral environmental agreements and more than 25 regional environmental regimes (Funke 2005). Moreover, a significant amount of foreign assistance money flowed to the Russian state to facilitate environmental protection during the 1990s: paying for environmental improvements in Russia often appears to be a relatively cost-effective measure for neighbouring countries to combat transboundary environmental problems (Darst 2001). Also foreign NGOs, business actors and investors are important actors in the Russian environmental sector.

LEGAL AND ADMINISTRATIVE FRAMEWORK FOR ENVIRONMENTAL POLICY

The evolution of Russian environmental governance inevitably reflects the more general societal changes, economic development and political reforms that have unfolded since the collapse of the Soviet Union (see Kulyasova and Kulyasov 2002; Aksenova 2006). Recent decades have seen significant reorganization of the Russian environmental administration. Environmental policy became institutionalized when the State Committee of Environmental Protection and Natural Resources [*Goskomekologiya*] was upgraded to a ministry,[6] and with the enactment of the Law on the Protection of the Environment in 1991. Decentralization of environmental policy in the late 1990s led to a rather heterogeneous system of environmental governance: combined with the Soviet tradition of industrial management and political leadership with strong regional elites, decentralization allowed the regions to act free of federal government control (Kotov and Nikitina 1996).

In tandem with President Putin's determination to strengthen the vertical of power and the ensuing reorganization of state administrative structure (see, for example, Morozov 2008), environmental administration as a whole was transferred to the Ministry of Natural Resources in 2000. Although the reorganization was justified in terms of enabling better allocation of responsibilities between federal, regional and local administrative bodies, it led to the weakening of federal environmental administration. For instance, the number of environmental inspectors declined dramatically (Henry and Douhovnikoff 2008, p. 440).

At the federal level, the administrative reform of 2004 clarified the mandates for environmental administration, separating the policy-making, regulatory and compliance-monitoring and service-provision functions of government authorities. Today, the key authorities responsible for formulating and implementing environmental policy and law at the federal level are the Ministry of Natural Resources and Environment, and the Federal Environmental, Industrial, and Nuclear Supervision Service [*Rostechnadzor*]. The former coordinates and supervises the activities of the Federal Service for Hydrometeorology and Environmental Monitoring [*Rosgidromet*], the Federal Service for Supervision of Natural

Resource Management [*Rosprirodnadzor*], the Federal Agency for Water Resources [*Rosvodresursy*], Federal Forest Agency [*Rosleshoz*], and the Federal Agency for Subsoil Management [*Rosnedra*]. The latter carries out functions on the adoption of environmental regulations, control and supervision, reporting directly to the government. Moreover, environmental functions have been assigned to many line ministries, among them the Ministry of Health and Social Development, the Ministry of Economic Development, and the Ministry of Industry and Trade. This means they are responsible for the preparation of wider policies which generate environmental impacts.

A major reformation of focused environmental legislation is currently underway: eight draft laws have in recent years been prepared by the Ministry of the Natural Resources and the Environment and are now at various stages of approval. These laws concern protected nature territories, protection of the marine environment from oil pollution, waste management, environmental impact assessment, environmental auditing and certain economic incentives for environmental protection.[7]

In summary, the institutional framework of environmental management in Russia today appears unstable, and has undergone numerous and contradictory changes. This has led to low levels of commitment to improve environmental policy and regulation, among managers at all levels (see OECD 2006, p. 10). Further, environmental policies often suffer from a lack of adequate financing over the state budget (see, for example, Henry and Douhovnikoff 2008).

In Russia, policy goals are often announced as presidential degrees [*ukaz*], with no further elaboration of the policy instruments to be used. Such tools commonly follow in the format of federal laws [*federalnyj zakon*], which require approval by the Duma. These tend to be the vehicle for establishing field-specific policy frameworks and the main choice of policy instruments. (See Nysten-Haarala 2000 for a more detailed typology of Russian legal instruments.) Ministries and/or other federal level authorities then prepare the practical rules for policy instruments and propose arrangements for monitoring as well as enforcement; such detailed elements are typically adopted in the form of government or ministerial level orders and decrees [*prikaz, rasporyazhenie*] etc.

As in all administrative systems, the legal instruments in Russia leave room for the interpretation and practices of the authority responsible. In addition, significant space for administrative corruption has remained endemic (Olimpieva 2010). Struggles over the promising territories of such 'corruption markets' between ministries and agencies typically lead to deadlocks in policy planning and in lower-level regulatory processes, especially if no strong political preferences have been signalled from the top level. Even 'state capture' – powerful industrial actors influencing the formation of legislation to their own advantage by providing private benefits to public officials – was widespread during the presidency of Boris Yeltsin, when the oligarchs gained power in the policy-making system (Hellman et al. 2000; Omelyanchuk 2001). However, Putin turned this trend during his first years in office, with his famous consolidation of power which resulted in a new social contract between the political leadership and the powerful industrialists. That said, state companies like Gazprom have remained powerful forces behind decision-making – in policy influence as well as ability to obstruct the implementation of adopted policies they disapprove of.

Also capacity issues complicate policy implementation, especially control and monitoring. The lack of data makes it difficult to establish objective baselines for policy goals or monitor performance during implementation, regardless of strict environmental regulations. Lack of data has also hampered the introduction of new environmental policy instruments like market-based tools (Kochtcheeva 2009, p.12). Accordingly, as Kochtcheeva notes (ibid., p.3), Russian environmental policy is based on regulatory and moral suasion rather than more flexible market-based approaches.

RUSSIA'S FOREIGN POLICY APPROACHES

Debating Parameters

The debating parameters over Russia's national identity and core goals of its foreign policy are rooted in several elements of the national history (see Kuchins and Zevelev 2012). First and foremost, there is the belief that Russia is a great power and must be treated as such: Russia's quest for the status of a great power within the confines of the state system has been an ongoing concern since the times of Peter the Great. The second element, intertwining with the first, includes the view of international politics as being Darwinian or Hobbesian by nature: competition and state-centric power politics is the dominant paradigm characterizing international relations. Alongside these two elements, the debating parameters are rooted in the still ongoing 200-year-old debate concerning the suitability of Western liberalism to Russia, and the extent to which Russia should engage with the West in order to 'catch up' in economic, technological and military development.

Since the early nineteenth century, Europe has emerged as a prism through which these parameters have been viewed: Europe has formed a defining 'constituting other' of the Russian identity (see Neumann 1996). Romantic nationalists gathered under the banner of 'Slavophilism' to oppose Western civilization and emphasize the unique character of Russian civilization based on Slavic Orthodox traditions. Those who looked to Europe for political and economic guidance came to be known as 'Westernizers'.

This schism has been evident in Russian foreign policy ever since – also in modern studies, like Tsygankov's (2010) categories of Westernism, statism and civilizationism. Whereas the first and last of these basically replicate the old divide between Westernizers and Slavophiles, 'statism' is characterized by pragmatism and the promotion of a strong state with multi-centrism. Along the same lines, based on an analysis of Russia's foreign policy views and the programmes of various political parties, groups, leading think tanks and experts, Kuchins and Zevelev (2012) sum up the current three major perspectives concerning main global trends and how Russian foreign policy should be formed as follows: (1) pro-Western liberals, who advocate close ties with Europe and the US and see Western market democracies as a model for reforming Russia's political system; (2) great power balancers, who promote a more multi-vectored foreign policy not so closely linked to domestic economic and political developments, interpreting the dynamics of the international system as more state-centric and focusing on Russian national interests in the context of the balance of power; and (3) nationalists, who tend to ascribe to Russia a special mission, especially towards its neighbours of the former Soviet Union. While these categories are more or less ideal types, these perspectives are evident in the domestic debate over Russia's foreign policy goals and are clearly reflected in Russia's behaviour in international politics.

For the purposes of this book, it is important to note that pro-Western liberals share the idea of Russia as a great power with the two other perspectives, but believe that the great power role does not necessarily entail any decrease in the status of the West: the two can coexist (Kuchins and Zevelev 2012, p.150; see also Makarychev and Morozov 2011). The great power balancers, in turn, hold that the West has been overplaying its role and should cede some of it to Russia. Yet, as Kuchins and Zevelev (2012) emphasize, they do not reject Western experience. Indeed, they are eager to learn from the West: they support importing Western technology, attract direct foreign investment, and compete successfully with the West. The main difference from the pro-Western liberals is that the great power balancers take for granted the existence of 'polarity' and power games on the global arena.

Recently, the concept of 'soft power' [*myahkaya sila*] (Nye 2004) has entered the vocabulary of Russian foreign policy. It has been explained that Russia's historically persistent desire to be recognized as a civilized nation (see Baburin and Nebrenchin 2009) acts as an impetus for conducting soft power efforts on the international arena (see Tsygankov 2013). Russia has launched several initiatives to promote its soft power – like the Valdai process for the world's top leaders, outreach to Western media, and the *Russkij Mir* [Russian World] Foundation that focuses on promoting Russian culture and language abroad (Chatham House 2011). According to Tsygankov (2013), Moscow's soft power is already considerable, particularly in Eurasia, but needs further development in order to project a clearer vision and a confident moral authority (see also Saari 2014).

Environmental arguments presented by Russian leaders, at home and abroad, are clearly part of such soft power efforts. With environmental argumentation, the values involved are attractive, since they are shared with Western audiences. Russia's environmental 'attraction' has also a concrete basis in the country's abundant natural resources – giving a substantial core for the discourse of 'Russia as an ecological donor'. However, as long as Russia also remains the world's largest producer of hydrocarbons, environmental arguments appear somewhat ambiguous and do not necessarily result in practical measures. Further, the way Russia has presented its eco-donor discourse ('we want compensation!') is more a matter of hard power means, not soft power ones. Andonova and Alexieva (2012, p. 625) provide a model-based example of the interplay between Russia's hard and soft power measures in international climate negotiations: Russia uses hard power measures more often than soft power measures, and on average Russia uses hard power measures more often than the Umbrella Group.[8]

Foreign Policy Visions of the Leadership

Domestic bargaining about foreign policy goals is limited in Russia, implying that the visions of the highest leadership usually dominate Russia's behaviour in international politics. Thus, we must examine the evolution of the dominant approaches of the leadership to Russia's foreign policy. According to Tsygankov (2010), immediately after the breakup of the Soviet Union, under Foreign Minister Andrey Kozyrev (1992–95), the explicit aim of Russian foreign policy was to learn from the West in introducing a market economy and a Western-type democracy. Becoming part of the West overshadowed the traditional image of Russia as a great power, and the transition to a market democracy became a major foreign policy goal, even trumping the preservation of sovereignty (Kuchins and Zevelev 2012, p. 149).

This Westernism was gradually replaced by a more statist approach, with elements of civilizationism, under Yevgeniy Primakov (foreign minister 1996–98, prime minister 1998–99). In the latter half of the 1990s, then, multilateralism, the balance of power and alliances eastwards with China and India became new hallmarks of Russian foreign policy. Disappointment with the West accumulated over several issues, including the wars in Kosovo and Chechnya. As Makarychev and Morozov (2011, p. 353) note, this destroyed the remnants of trust in the West and, together with rising oil prices and the upturn in the Russian economy, paved the way for more assertive foreign policy. When Vladimir Putin came to power in 2000, the statist approach was cultivated further: Russian foreign policy became characterized by pragmatism, the use of trade and economy as main instruments of foreign policy, as well as certain elements of great power thinking. This thinking was defined by slogans like 'strengthening the Russian state' and 'dictatorship of the law' (Glinski 2000). During the Medvedev presidency, foreign policy was increasingly seen by the leadership as a means of facilitating domestic change and overall modernization project of the Russian economy (see Henry and McIntosh Sundstrom 2012, p. 1317).

Under Putin's second presidency, Russia's approach to foreign policy has seemed all but clear-cut. Kuchins and Zevelev (2012, p. 159) note that, at least rhetorically, Medvedev placed himself among the pro-Western liberals, whereas the 'second' Putin seems to belong more to the great power balancers. For example, in his article on Russia's foreign policy published shortly before the March 2012 presidential elections, Putin referred to foreign policy as a derived function of domestic policy, implying that the major aim of Russia's foreign policy is to advance the internal development of the country (*Moskovskie Novosti*, 27 February 2012). According to Putin's foreign policy vision, the preservation of the global balance of power and the pre-eminence of international law and national sovereignty are important goals, as well as control of the use of soft power.[9] Priority is to be given to improving the country's image abroad.

The new foreign policy concept, introduced in February 2013, underlines Russia's increased responsibility for setting the international agenda and shaping the system of international relations as the general provisions for its own foreign policy. Two basic goals are stated: 'ensuring the security of the country, protecting and strengthening its sovereignty and territorial integrity and securing its high standing in the international community as one of the influential and competitive poles of the modern world'; and 'creating favourable external conditions for a steady and dynamic growth of the Russian economy and its technological modernization with a view to putting it on innovation-based development tracks, as well as for improving the quality of life, strengthening the rule of law and democratic institutions, and ensuring human rights and freedoms.' Both great power balancing and economic alliancing with the West can be discerned here. The concept of soft power is also emphasized: '"(s)oft power", a comprehensive toolkit for achieving foreign policy objectives building on civil society potential, information, cultural and other methods and technologies alternative to traditional diplomacy, is becoming an indispensable component of modern international relations.' [10]

Events in Ukraine in 2014 have, however, made most of the above sound like empty rhetoric. As the evolution of Russia's foreign policy during the last two decades has shown, what are seen as Russia's national interests may change unpredictably, depending first and foremost on the global economy (see Kuchins and Zevelev 2012, p. 160). First, we should bear in mind, as Averre (2008, p. 28) argues, that official documents like the foreign policy concept reflect what the leaders want to *present* as a set of objective ideas about Russia's approach to external relations. To what extent these documents actually guide policies is, however, open to debate, as Russia's foreign policy is in practice often inconsistent. Second, as noted by Tsygankov (2012, p. 709), Russia has throughout history followed not one but several distinct trajectories in its external relations, depending on the context.

Any foreign policy action is a social phenomenon – which in turn implies that it cannot be fully understood without exploring the surrounding context (see Hopf 2002; Pouliot 2007; also Tsygankov 2014). In the following chapters, we analyse specific debates on Russia's international environmental policy objectives and their meaning by studying how Russians themselves have reasoned about the issues at hand, seeking to explicate the discourses and their linkages to the specific foreign and domestic policy contexts.

NOTES

1. This section draws on Andresen et al. (2012).
2. One of the primary foundations of the precautionary principle, and globally accepted definitions, results from the work of the Rio Conference, or 'Earth Summit' in 1992. Principle #15 of the Rio Declaration notes: 'In order to protect the environment, the precautionary approach shall be widely applied by States according to their capabilities. Where there are threats of serious or irreversible damage, lack of full scientific certainty shall not be used as a reason for postponing cost-effective measures to prevent environmental degradation.'
3. These general environmental policy initiatives and laws include the Presidential decree 'Concept for the transition of the Russian Federation to sustainable development' (1996), a federal target programme 'Ecology and natural resources of Russia 2002–2010' (2001), Federal Law 'On environmental protection' (2002), Ecological Doctrine of the Russian Federation (2002), the 'Concept of long-term socio-economic

development of the Russian Federation for the period up to the year 2020' (2008) and 'Principles of State policy in the area of environmental development of the Russian Federation for the period up to the year 2030' (2012).

4. Ministry of Economic Development of the Russian Federation (2011), 'Projection of long-term social and economic development of the Russian Federation until 2030', available at: www.economy.gov.ru/minec/activity/sections/macro/prognoz/doc20130325_06 (accessed 10 June 2014).

5. For example, President of Russia (2010), 'Consolidated state policy is needed to address environmental problems', speech of President Dmitry Medvedev at a State Council Presidium on 27 May 2010, available at: http://eng.kremlin.ru/news/273 (accessed 11 April 2014).

6. In 1996, the ministry was reassigned the status of a State Committee, and many of its tasks were transferred to the Ministry of Natural Resources.

7. For example, *Russian Sustainability Newsletter* (2013), 3 (March): 2, available at: www.geogr.msu.ru/science/projects/our/ross_swed/NewsLETTER/3_13.pdf (accessed 15 April 2014).

8. A negotiation grouping in the climate negotiations which consists of Australia, Canada, Iceland, Japan, New Zealand, Norway, Russia, Ukraine, and US.

9. 'Soft power' can be defined as the attractiveness of a country's international image which consists of their value system, political system, economic order, culture, traditions, ideology, religion, etc. (see Nye 2004).

10. This quote and immediately above, The Ministry of Foreign Affairs of the Russian Federation (2013), 'Concept of the Foreign Policy of the Russian Federation', available at: www.mid.ru/brp_4.nsf/0/76389FEC168189ED44257B2E0039B16D (accessed 9 June 2014).

3.   The global case: the climate regime

INTRODUCTION

Climate change is one of the main challenges facing mankind in the twenty-first century. Industrialization – first in the Organisation for Economic Co-operation and Development (OECD) countries and the Soviet bloc, and later on in the emerging economies in Asia – has triggered unpredictable changes, forecast to generate an average increase in global temperature of some 1.8°C to 4.0°C by the end of this century (IPCC 2007). These changes are expected to lead to droughts, floods, melting of the Arctic, sea level rise, as well as extreme weather events. In line with the trend of addressing regional and global environmental problems through multilateral environmental agreements since the 1970s, the issue was elevated to the global agenda in the 1980s.

In order to tackle climate change, the UN Framework Convention on Climate Change was adopted in 1992, followed by its Kyoto Protocol in 1997. The former describes the problem of climate change and broadly defines the task at hand, as well as the principles to guide international cooperation in tackling the problem. The latter represents a step forward, establishing legally binding targets to reduce or limit the greenhouse gas emissions of industrialized countries in the Annex I group in comparison to 1990 emissions levels,[1] and their responsibility for financially assisting the non-Annex I group of developing countries with climate mitigation and adaptation actions.

This chapter analyses the storylines and discourses related to Russian climate politics and policies. The material is drawn from Russian domestic debates around the adoption of the Kyoto Protocol in 2004 and the rejection of its second commitment period in 2012, and the related decisions in putting Joint Implementation – one of the Kyoto mechanisms – into practice in Russia. The aim is to provide insights into the starting points and shared assumptions of the Russian actors on the issue of climate change and the implications to related international cooperation. Most of the material used has been collected from the media, partly using the Integrum database; also some policy documents have been consulted. Additionally, interviews have provided background material, although no interviews were conducted specifically for this analysis.

BACKGROUND

The Regime

The Kyoto Protocol is a sophisticated multilateral environmental agreement that consists of not only legally binding targets (listed in its Annex B) relative to 1990 level emissions, which are converted into emissions allowances, or quotas, but also an arrangement for calculating the contributions of carbon sinks (absorption of greenhouse gases from the atmosphere by land use, land use change and forestry activities), and a compliance system for monitoring target achievement. In addition came the Kyoto mechanisms – market-based tools which provide flexibility for implementing these targets where it is most economically effective. International emissions trading allows Annex I industrialized countries to trade their quotas; joint implementation (JI) allows this trading to be linked to concrete emissions-reduction projects in the selling industrialized country; and the Clean Development Mechanism enables non-Annex I countries to host emissions-reduction projects and sell verified quotas to industrialized countries.

The first Kyoto commitment period extended from 2008 to 2012, and some of the Annex I countries adopted further targets for the second commitment period, 2013–20. The original idea of the Protocol was to establish a permanent regime which would update the stringency and geographical coverage of national emissions-reduction commitments over time for subsequent commitment periods after the first commitment period, 2008–12. This was to be guided by the development of countries as well as of climate science as reported by the Intergovernmental Panel on Climate Change (IPCC). However, already the first commitment period encountered problems when the largest emitter – the US – withdrew from the pact. Some industrialized countries adopted further targets for the second commitment period, but it had already become obvious that the pact could not serve as the main international tool for tackling climate change, since the US as well as major emerging economies now responsible for most of the global emissions growth were not prepared to adopt legally binding targets under the regime. The negotiation process for a new more globally inclusive agreement was launched in Durban in 2011 and is scheduled to be finalized by 2015.

Russia and Climate

Russia has emerged as a major player in international climate politics due to its decisive role in the entry into force of the Kyoto Protocol, its position as a major global supplier of fossil fuels and its significant share of global emissions (fourth largest, with the share of some 5 per cent)[2] – Russia's greenhouse gas emissions declined significantly as a result of the post-Soviet economic transition which closed down much of the highly-emitting, obsolete industrial production capacity for good. Also the slow improvement in energy efficiency in the economy has contributed to limiting emissions growth, which stood at an average of 1.1 per cent per annum from 1999 to 2011.[3] As a result, Russia's emissions remained 31 per cent below the 1990 level in 2011. Figure 3.1 shows emission trends in Russia for those years.

The most important elements of the Protocol for Russia include its unambitious target during the first commitment period, the Kyoto mechanisms and the forest carbon sinks. The fact that the surplus quotas created by the post-Soviet emission collapse were tradable opened for Russia the possibility of receiving significant sums from their sales. In practice, the options were either direct sales of allowances through international emissions trading, or sales linked to individual emission reduction projects through JI. Emissions trading gained Russian interest initially, but JI

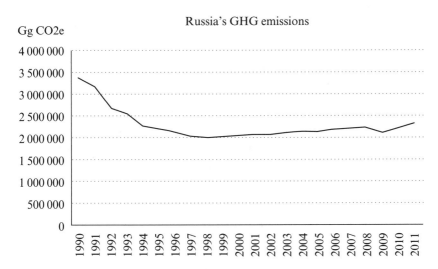

Source: http://unfccc.int/di/DetailedByParty.do.

Figure 3.1   Russia's GHG emissions

later grew in importance when the expected main buyer, the US, withdrew from the Protocol. The remaining potential buyers, Japan, Canada and especially the EU, were more concerned about the environmental reputation of the Russian surplus quotas, in particular their permanence.[4] As a result, there was more demand for quotas through JI, which ensures the permanence of quotas by linking them to specific projects.

Also, forest carbon sinks are relevant to Russia as a forest-rich country. Article 3.3 allows net changes in emissions by sources and removals by sinks through direct human-induced land use, land use change and forestry activities, limited to afforestation, reforestation and deforestation since 1990, to be used to meet the emissions-reduction commitments of industrialized countries. Article 3.4 allows these countries to select additional human-induced activities related to land use, land use change and forestry specifically (forest management, cropland management, grazing land management and re-vegetation) to be included in their accounting; however, these were limited by national maximum limits during the first commitment period, due to calculation uncertainties (Höhne et al. 2007). Russia has been promoting the maximal inclusion of activities under Art. 3.4, and has opposed politically allocated quotas to these activities.

The cases of decision-making as to Russian participation in the Kyoto Protocol, and the implementation of JI in Russia, are quite diverse as regards participants, the international as well as domestic attention gained, and their extension over time. The first debate was intensified by Russia's decisive role in the entry into force of the Kyoto Protocol. As a result, Russia was subjected to intense international lobbying and media scrutiny for over a year in 2003 and 2004. Later, however, discussion on participation in the second Kyoto commitment period was significantly less intense and mostly domestic: the pact had already lost its political momentum, as many important parties had opted out, making Russian participation significantly less relevant the second time around. Debates on JI were mostly domestic, and involved the private sector. The discussion prior to the first commitment period (2005–07) had been more abstract than the debate during the first commitment period (2009–12) when JI was already being implemented.

RATIFICATION AND PARTICIPATION, KYOTO SECOND COMMITMENT PERIOD

Russia has considered its participation in the Kyoto Protocol twice so far: first, with ratification of the pact in 2003–04, and then taking a further commitment for the second commitment period in 2011–12. This section presents the dominant storylines used during these processes, and compares the developments of the argumentation.

Storylines on Ratification of the Kyoto Protocol 2003–04

In order to enter into force, the Kyoto Protocol required ratification by 55 countries accounting for 55 per cent of the Annex I (industrialized countries) members' greenhouse gas emissions in 1990. As the US had rejected participation, thereby excluding 25 per cent of the total emissions, the Protocol could not enter into force without Russia's 17 per cent share of the total emissions from Annex I industrialized countries. This put Russia in the international media spotlight. Finally, Russia ratified the Kyoto Protocol in 2004, after a long domestic debate and bargaining process with other – pro-Kyoto – parties.[5]

The debate prior to ratification by the Duma in October 2004 reflected the views of the opposition. The official presentations of the issue by Alexander Bedritsky, head of the environmental monitoring agency Roshydromet, and Vladimir Gratchev, head of the Duma Ecological Committee, both took a positive stance toward ratification, delivering the messages of ministerial as well as Duma Ecological Committee preparatory processes. However, only one of 16 deputies who took the floor was supportive of ratification. In the end, ratification was achieved with the support of 74.2 per cent of the deputies in the Duma dominated by President Putin's party.

Storyline I: a political pact with only benefits to Russia
The main storyline that supported ratification presented the Kyoto Protocol as a favourable deal for Russia because it involved few obligations – 'not much is required from Russia'[6] – and granted access to financial as well as political benefits. JI was seen as a potential source of modernization investments, although this was recognized as dependent on domestic implementation.[7] It was argued that the regime posed no economic threat to Russia, because overshooting the first commitment period target was considered unrealistic,[8] and that modernization of industry through JI would support economic growth in the longer term.[9] This was seen to be the direction the Russian economy should take in any case; for instance diversification of the economy in favour of manufacturing industry away from energy exports was mentioned.[10] It was also seen to be in line with President Putin's goal of doubling gross domestic product (GDP): it was argued that this would not be possible with the current level of energy intensity, and that emissions-reduction measures could help by lowering energy intensity along with emissions.[11] Some went even as far as to say that the benefits offered were so good that Russia should ratify even if

science were wrong about climate change.[12] It was also considered possible to limit the threat of uncontrolled emissions trading by domestic actors, which was feared by some opponents.[13]

Another important set of arguments for ratification under this storyline concerned the foreign policy benefits. Supporters underscored how bringing the Kyoto regime into force could boost Russia's image in the international arena as a 'civilized' country, and even an 'environmental leader', while rejecting the pact could lead to loss of trust by the international community.[14] Regardless, these 'environmental' arguments seemed mostly driven by the concerns of other countries, and thus playing along with them. Even though the importance of the environmental focus of the pact was part of the official ratification discussion, it seemed more like lip service, as the issue was generally ignored in the domestic media debate. As a response to arguments from the scientific community that the Kyoto Protocol was ineffective (see below), one of the 'buzz lines' under this storyline was that the pact is only the first step towards solving the problem of climate change.[15] The EU's support to Russian membership in the World Trade Organization (WTO) provided non-environment related foreign policy benefits, and has been seen as an important factor supporting ratification[16] – although some in Russia blamed the EU for not respecting this deal as agreed by the 'gentlemen's agreement'.[17] Oddly enough, several officials denied that there was any link between Kyoto ratification and WTO membership.[18]

The main voices within this storyline were Roshydromet's Bedritsky and the Duma Ecological Committee's Gratchev, which officially led preparations for ratification, as well as other ministries involved (Ministry of Economic Development, Ministry of Industry and Energy), climate policy experts like Viktor Danilov-Danylian, and representatives of what was then the electricity monopoly RAO UES Rossii.

Storyline II: threats to and conspiracy against Russia
One group of those opposed to ratification argued that Russia's emissions would exceed the Kyoto limit of 1990 levels during the first commitment period (2008–12).[19] This, it was feared, would slow down economic growth, by putting limits to industrial activities or leading to costs because of the need to purchase additional emissions allowances to top up Russia's emission allocations to accommodate economic growth in the future.[20] President Putin's goal of doubling GDP was considered to be in jeopardy. Presidential adviser Andrey Illarionov used emotive language, for instance calling Kyoto 'the pact of death' which – in his view– aimed at suffocating economic growth in countries that took on commitments.[21]

Opponents also questioned whether there would be sufficient benefits available from the Kyoto mechanisms, since the expected main buyer of Russian allowances, the US, had withdrawn and there was no other 'guaranteed' demand for Russian emissions allowances,[22] in terms of volumes or quota prices.[23] It was argued that 'nobody has concretely said that they would buy our quotas'.[24] The true nature of the net benefits available was also questioned, because of the costs of modernization required for Kyoto compliance, expected to be much higher than funds available from the Kyoto mechanisms,[25] and the above mentioned lack of demand for Russian quotas.[26] One Duma deputy put into words a feeling that was perhaps shared by others under this storyline: Kyoto consists merely of 'empty promises' to Russia.[27] Also, the calls for guarantees indicate that something was expected, but with reservations.

There were also conspiracy theories. Doubts were cast on JI benefits, and there was talk of sinister goals behind the scheme, inside and outside Russia. It was feared that domestic industrial actors would rush to sell Russia's quotas for short-term benefits, thereby removing future headroom for economic growth.[28] It was sometimes claimed that Anatoly Chubais, with the electricity monopoly RAO UES Rossii he headed at the time, was pulling strings behind the leadership. He was said to aim at uncontrolled sales of quotas, or even taking over quotas and later selling them back to the government ('privatization of the atmosphere').[29]

Also the goals of foreigners were questioned.[30] International oversight of emissions, and thus industrial activities, was seen as increasing control over Russia. One goal of the Kyoto regime was said to be to gain access to Russia's natural resources. For instance, it was claimed that foreign governments would seek to buy energy from Russia, whereas Russia would end up paying for the pollution caused by generating this energy.[31] Further, fears were expressed that, by joining the Protocol, Russia might become dependent on access to foreign technologies, as the most efficient technologies would have to be imported (Roginko 2002). The Kyoto regime was thus presented as a commercial and not an environmental pact. Some even saw it as a green conspiracy, or a form of colonialism, where foreign interests would reap commercial benefits by marketing technologies to Russia.[32]

The EU was seen as the main conspirator, and its environmental motivations as a promoter of the Kyoto regime were questioned. Trying to identify the 'real' reason behind the EU's climate policy, Roginko (2002) argued: 'nobody believes that the EU can divert tens of billions of euros to solving a problem which . . . will cause problems only in about hundred years, not before'. His suggestion was that the EU's motivation was to ensure markets for the profitable European 'eco' industry. One Duma deputy called climate change itself 'a media myth maintained by the EU'.[33]

The main voices in this storyline belonged to presidential economic adviser Illarionov, some top politicians, like Prime Minister Fradkov, and various State Duma deputies.

Storyline III: ineffective pact without scientific basis

Another line of argumentation against the Protocol criticized the document for lacking 'scientific basis', as it would not limit concentrations of greenhouse gases in the atmosphere sufficiently to solve the problem of climate change.[34] It was even considered to have no positive environmental impact.[35] This line of argumentation was seen as an environmental – or 'ecological', to use the Russian equivalent – argument. The anthropogenic nature of climate change as a phenomenon was challenged by many,[36] and the potential of positive impacts of climate change to Russia instead of negative ones was strongly held.[37] Putin himself famously joked at the World Climate Change Conference, organized in Moscow in 2003: 'If climate gets warmer in Russia, then we wouldn't need to spend so much money on fur hats.'[38] Domestically, companies and officials involved in the preparations for the Kyoto mechanisms were argued to have forgotten climate itself while focusing on the economic opportunities provided by the Kyoto mechanisms.[39]

The 'ineffectiveness' of the pact also concerned its low global coverage.[40] Russia's commitments – which were seen to limit economic development – were considered discriminatory[41] since the US and major emerging economies were not taking on equivalent burdens.[42]

It was even argued that Russia should be recognized as an 'ecological donor', referring to the carbon that Russia's forests were considered to contain and absorb from the atmosphere. Compensation was presented as a fair claim against this 'ecological service', insufficiently reflected in the Protocol.[43] This was linked to the calculation of forest sinks. Benefit sharing through sinks allocations (para 3.4) was seen as unfair or even discriminatory,[44] as it was based on political negotiation rather than scientific analysis. Some even argued that since Russia played such a crucial role for the entry into force of the Protocol, Moscow should demand more 'privileges', such as higher forest sinks allocations.[45]

Main voices in this storyline were academicians Yuri Izrael and Kirill Kondratev. Also some Duma deputies were very vocal about the lack of participation, and the inadequate recognition of Russia's contributions.

Storylines on Participation: Kyoto Second Period 2011–12

As neither the US nor the leading emerging economies of China and India showed signs of taking on commitments for the second commitment period, Japan, Canada and Russia also rejected further commitments for 2013–20. The EU, Norway, Switzerland and Australia took on commitments largely for political reasons, as the G77 group of developing countries sees the pact, and its principle of common but differentiated responsibilities, as a symbol of industrialized countries taking the lead in mitigating the climate change to which their industrialization has contributed so heavily.

Already in 2011 the Russian leadership stated that the country would not be taking on commitments under the second commitment period.[46] Internationally, Russia's participation was far less relevant to the success of the pact this time than in the case of ratification. Also the withdrawal of other industrialized countries perhaps paved the way for this decision, and the main focus was on the future global deal to be negotiated by 2015. The major dilemma with Russian withdrawal concerned participation in the Kyoto mechanisms, especially in JI. The domestic debate in 2012 was mostly between top policy-makers and project developers keen to continue receiving money from selling quotas from projects, thus wanting to change the initial position.

Storyline I: economic benefits without burdensome commitments

A coalition consisting of the economic wing of the government ministries, Sberbank and companies involved in JI projects as well as NGOs pushed for Russian participation in the second Kyoto commitment period, arguing 'there is no reason for Russia to drop out of the Protocol: tangible economic benefits are there, but burdensome commitments not'.[47] It was argued that continuous investments in modernization projects would be available through JI if Russia signed up to the Kyoto second phase; otherwise, Russian actors would no longer have access to the international JI market. Furthermore, receiving these revenues was not considered to require significant work, whereas rejection would mean economic loss given the work already put in developing a domestic system for project approval.[48] Russian rejection of the Kyoto second phase was described as 'buying a train ticket and then deciding to walk' – referring to abandoning a financial opportunity that had been established through considerable effort.[49]

The significance of investments received was emphasized by the beneficiaries – industrial units which financed shares of their modernization by selling quotas generated through JI.[50] The multiplier effect of JI investments covering only about 20 per cent of project costs, and thus, attracting significant investments from domestic sources, was also noted as an advantage in terms of tax revenues.[51] As a linked side argument, it was pointed out that Russia's export industry could become vulnerable to carbon protectionism if the country dropped out of the international carbon regulatory system:[52] other countries might justify protectionist actions based on their more stringent environmental policy if Russia did not regulate carbon emissions.

The second commitment period was also seen as not involving any economic risks to Russia, as the analysis quoted by the Ministry of Economic Development showed that emissions would remain significantly below the Kyoto base-year 1990 until 2020. This source also forecast that emissions would start declining, down to 30–50 per cent below 1990 level by 2050.[53] In addition, further emissions-reduction projects through JI, especially energy-efficiency improvements, were seen as contributing to this trend of declining emissions.

Storyline II: low coverage and lack of economic benefits justifies dropping out

Many Russian actors did not consider the second phase of Kyoto effective in terms of limiting emissions to the atmosphere: in the absence of the US, China and India, it covers only 15 per cent of global emissions. The official position, articulated by Vice-Premier Arkady Dvorkovich, was that Russia would take on commitments under the Kyoto second phase if leading economies did likewise.[54] Otherwise, dropping out of the pact was deemed justified: Russia could withdraw from Kyoto with a 'clear conscience'.[55] However, domestic commitments were introduced as an alternative to the second period commitments, most probably for image reasons.[56]

It was feared that taking on commitments under these circumstances could compromise the international competitiveness of Russian industry.[57] Rejection of the Kyoto second period was seen as having environmental foundations as well.[58] For instance, Bedritsky, now the climate envoy to the Russian President, argued: 'continuation of the Kyoto Protocol is a false goal which detracts attention away from solutions to real problems'.[59] Indeed, some even pointed him out as the 'only opponent' to the second Kyoto period.[60]

Both the lack of demand for emission reductions from the Russian JI and their low market prices were used as arguments to question the benefits available through JI. The revenues available were seen as small, given the scale of the Russian economy. The arguments supporting the adoption of the second period of Kyoto were seen as commercial group interests of the companies and agencies involved in JI, who had been maintaining the carbon market as their real concern. Their hopes for access to the EU Emissions Trading Scheme through JI were dismissed as illusory.[61]

Development of Argumentation between 2004 and 2012

Most of the arguments supporting and opposing the second Kyoto commitment period were similar to those used during the ratification debate. Benefits were the leading – and unquestioned – theme in both debates; and the opposing and supporting sides accepted this as a starting point for discussion. Gains were seen as a legitimate expectation in exchange of participating in, and thus supporting, the regime. The lack of what was considered as sufficient benefits was similarly seen as a legitimate reason for not participating. However, the tone changed to some extent between 2004 and 2012. By 2012 there was no longer talk of 'guaranteed benefits', although it could still be read between the lines that EU policies against purchasing Russian quotas under the second commitment period were seen as unfair market manipulation.

The main argument against Kyoto was the lack of participation by other major emitters, and the consequences as regards the 'efficiency' of the regime as well as its expected impacts on Russian competitiveness, in both 2004 and 2012. In the case of the second commitment period, the issue was even more acute, as a larger number of countries had dropped out, and none of the major emerging economies had taken on commitments as originally expected. Geopolitics can thus be seen as the underlying factor in both decisions. In 2004, however, this was articulated more clearly, mainly because of Russia's key role in bringing the pact into force. Image-related viewpoints had a central role in 2004 but their relevance had faded by 2012, probably due to Russia's less visible and non-decisive role in the process. However, declaring domestic commitments to 'replace' second commitment period targets provides evidence of at least some interest in maintaining Russia's international environmental reputation. Some Russian scientists still questioned the basis of climate science, and the lack of recognition of Russian forests under the regime was still seen as unfair in 2012, but these previously major points did not come up very often.

Interestingly, Bedritsky had shifted from being the main promoter of Kyoto ratification to the leading opponent of its second commitment period. This was probably linked to his position as presidential adviser in 2012 – but, given his expertise on the issue, also the actual context of the second period, with disappointment because the regime had failed to evolve as expected, could have played a role. Also the disappointments with JI during the first commitment period may have contributed to this change of heart.

Kyoto's environmental importance did not gain any significant role in the ratification debate in terms of impacts expected as a result of climate change. Also during the debate on the second period, the negative impacts of climate change on Russian territory were mentioned very rarely. However, the views labelled as 'ecological' in Russia were important. The leading argument against Kyoto second phase was its low coverage and thus its minuscule influence on the atmospheric concentrations of greenhouse gases. The early scepticism as to the scientific basis of climate change, and questioning the negative nature of the impacts of climate change would support this. But it can be argued that the lack of participation was seen as a geopolitical rather than an environmental issue. Many Russian actors seemed to also assume that other countries were not supporting the Protocol for environmental reasons. This had led to speculation as to what the underlying 'real' reasons could be, which in some cases led to conspiracy theories, especially during the ratification debate. Such arguments were fewer, more sophisticated and subtle by the time of the second commitment period debate. For instance, environmental argumentations were recognized as a motivation for technology standards, at the same time as they were seen as carbon protectionism.

In 2003 and 2004, the Protocol was still seen to be linked to 'promises' made to Russia. Opponents claimed that these were empty promises. Such an approach may sound strange, as the goal of any environmental pact is to solve the problem in question rather than to re-apportion benefits among participants. However, this may reflect the general Russian view of environmental pacts as an issue promoted by Western governments, and thus, worth compensation against supporting them. This was reflected in the disbelief expressed concerning the true nature of the environmental concerns of other governments. A price tag on Russia's support to the pact was in order, especially in the case of ratification. Interestingly, this seems to have changed by 2012: 'promises' or 'guarantees' were no longer called for. Now the discussion focused on more realistically estimating the expected benefits, to the Russian economy as well as to the atmosphere.

JOINT IMPLEMENTATION – EARLY PHASE AND IMPLEMENTATION PHASE COMPARISON

Under the Kyoto Protocol, Russia was entitled to participate in joint implementation during the first commitment period 2008–12. The main task of the domestic policy process was to establish an administrative framework for approval of JI projects in Russia. This process was prolonged. Even though discussions on JI began in Russia soon after the mechanism was adopted in 1997 as part of the Kyoto Protocol, and more detailed international rules and guidelines were specified in 2001, the actual process for establishing a domestic approval system was not launched until in 2005. Adjustments to the Russian JI regulations continued until 2011 – which left very little time for putting the mechanism into practice, as the first commitment period expired at the end of 2012. Early discussions (2004–05) took thus a different starting point – focusing on establishment of the approval system – than did discussions during project implementation phase (2010–12).

Storylines on the Early Phase of JI, 2004–05

During the observation period the administrative process of setting up JI was only starting, as Russian participation was still under discussion. Some pilot projects (Activities Implemented Jointly – for a detailed description, see Korppoo 2005) had been implemented in Russia, but experience of the mechanism was very limited otherwise. Various ideas on approaches to JI were discussed internationally, and some Russian actors were influenced by these discussions. As JI also played a role in the ratification discussion, some overlaps are inevitable between this section and the ratification discussion above. The circle of actors discussing the pros and cons expected from JI was much wider and had less experience of the mechanism, than after implementation had begun.

Storyline I: private sector leadership of JI: best opportunity to modernize technologies

Some private sector actors, especially the electricity monopoly RAO UES and its Energy Carbon Fund, argued that carbon market mechanisms, JI in particular, should be launched early – prior to the beginning of the first commitment period in 2008 – in order to make it easier to gain maximum financial benefits from the Protocol. The government was criticized for not ratifying Kyoto or establishing JI regulations to facilitate use of the mechanism. Companies successfully participating in tenders of foreign quota buyers showed that the bottleneck was the Russian government, which was not prepared to provide letters to guarantee the transfer of quotas to the foreign buyer prior to establishing a functional JI approval system at home.[62] The 'economic losses' due to this government non-action were often featured in headlines.[63]

Also emphasized was the importance of establishing a domestic emissions trading scheme, a voluntary system, as it was seen as enabling access to the newly established EU Emissions Trading Scheme, under which carbon prices were higher than in the international market. Private-sector actors made proposals as to how this could be done, and wanted to lead the process.[64] They argued that significant benefits could be achieved only by gaining access to the EU trading system.[65] The Ministry of Economic Development was in some cases supportive of these arguments.[66]

Storyline II: JI is an opportunity, state control obstructs private sector opportunism

Early arguments concerning JI from the state administration were often closely linked to their support for Kyoto ratification. Industry's need to modernize and replace old production technologies was recognized as having synergies with JI projects.[67] This was seen as a benefit that could be gained from Kyoto. Also environmental benefits from the emissions reductions generated by JI were recognized by the administration, at least on the level of argumentation.[68]

The readiness of projects waiting for approval was highlighted. However, the preparatory agencies were cautious about establishing a carbon market, and reluctant to facilitate an early start for JI that would have allowed more freedom to the private sector – which was probably better prepared for managing JI than the state administration. For instance, the Ministry of Industry and Energy called for a balanced approach, and denied that the matter was urgent.[69] JI was also seen as a more realistic option than emissions trading (perhaps due to the control it allowed over private sector activities through the legal basis for the process), and more likely to boost economic growth than direct trading of quotas.[70] But also the shortcomings of the administration itself were foreseen. Bedritsky, head of Roshydromet at the time, argued that Russia's benefits from the regime would depend on its implementation.[71]

Storyline III: JI sounds too good to be true

Some actors, especially many Duma deputies and Presidential adviser Illarionov, were sceptical to the potential benefits available from JI. The demand for Russian quotas was questioned, and guarantees called for. The beneficial impacts of the Kyoto mechanisms were expected to involve some kind of trick rather than provide genuine profits; as one Duma deputy put it, 'cheese is free only in a mouse trap'.[72]

The money from JI was considered as small, especially in comparison to the total costs of modernizing the Russian industry, which was expected to be required in order to comply with Kyoto commitments (Institut Ekonomicheskogo Analiza 2003). This was also linked to the view that one of the main motivations for some parties to support the regime was to make Russia and other countries dependent on their technology exports.[73] The participation of RAO UES, and especially its enthusiasm for leading in the management of the Kyoto mechanisms, was met with deep scepticism, and seen as a way for the private sector to grab more of the Russian national wealth.[74]

Storylines on JI, Implementation Phase 2009–12

During the period 2009–12, JI was being implemented in Russia. After the prolonged process of establishing domestic JI approval procedures, the private sector was beginning to see an inflow of investments through JI. The domestic procedures and the control entailed by them still limited the benefits available and maintained the uncertainty. Also the ministries and agencies involved were gaining experience of the mechanism, and the potential benefit streams available to them. The approaching end of the first commitment period, and the uncertainties linked to Russian participation in the second period – and thus, the future of JI in Russia – gave rise to major concern and disputes.

Storyline I: improve domestic administration to gain more from JI under Kyoto I by the end of 2012
Decision-makers and the presidential administration especially regarded JI as an opportunity, but saw its implementation failing because of shortcomings in the domestic bureaucratic system and the agencies involved. Attention focused on improving the performance of the domestic approval system so as to obtain maximum benefits during the first commitment period.[75] As noted by President Medvedev: '. . . the Kyoto Protocol was adopted with so much difficulty . . . Since we have signed it, we need to get some investment after all.' He went on to say that it was 'fair' for Russia to have received limited benefits as the domestic facilitation process was not of better quality.[76] Modernization and influential projects in terms of policy implementation, such as associated petroleum gas flaring cuts, were seen as desirable benefits that could be obtained through JI.[77] However, the investment flows were deemed small on the scale of the Russian economy, and decreasing quota prices were mentioned as one factor that made JI less attractive beyond 2012.[78]

Storyline II: Russian JI is legitimate and under control
The agencies leading JI, the Ministry of Economic Development and Sberbank, took the limited success of JI as a starting point for supporting the continuation of JI, even though they recognized that Russia could have benefited more through earlier action. Russia's actions on JI were considered as legitimate and in line with international guidelines. The environmental impact of JI projects and their acceptance by foreign buyers was emphasized.[79] The requirement of re-investing revenues from

JI into further environmental projects was considered as the ultimate proof of the 'green' nature of the projects, even though it was also admitted that some already implemented projects were 'converted' into JI projects.[80]

The urge to control JI participants was evident: project owners (companies) were required to be registered in Russia, and foreign partners could not submit applications to Sberbank. Project consultants were required to have an office in Russia, and Russia set up its own list of project verifiers instead of using the internationally approved one.[81] Further, project types were limited: a lucrative project type, gas distribution pipeline renovation, was excluded as it suffered from problems with environmental image; moreover, it would have channelled JI revenues to Russian project owners registered outside the country (Korppoo and Moe 2008).

Actors within this storyline supported the continuation of JI beyond 2012, and sought to find an approach that would suit the political leadership. They explored the possible use of JI during the 'true-up' period of the Kyoto Protocol until 2014–15[82] or participating in JI without quantitative commitments under the second period, as well as the feasibility of joining it.[83] Attempts to gain access to JI without taking on further commitments were rejected by the international community. Internally, using JI as a domestic offset scheme was also discussed.

Demand for Russian quotas during the second period was questioned, and foreign buyers were seen to 'discriminate' against Russian quotas in terms of prices paid. Some projects had contracted the quotas they expected to generate based on 'market price' rather than a fixed price[84] – and foreign buyers saw this as price manipulation.[85] The internal price in the EU Emissions Trading Scheme, which is created by different dynamics than that of international price for quotas, was routinely used as a reference for a 'fair price' for quotas.[86]

Storyline III: JI administration is getting better – it makes no sense to stop now

The private sector was more critical to the political leadership and the administration. In particular, the interest organization of businesses, the Union of Industrialists and Entrepreneurs, argued that the private sector required more support to make the most of JI in Russia, and that the bureaucracy and control around JI were at fault. In the beginning of the observation period, JI approval procedures were still under preparation, and the government was criticized for 'lost' profits.[87] Later on, criticism focused on the tendering system in project allocation and the limited amount of allowances reserved for JI by the government.[88] Companies cited problems with project allocation criteria: big state companies were seen to be favoured by the JI operator Sberbank, and its role as a monopolist seller of quotas was held to be unheard of and highly detrimental to attracting JI investments to Russia.[89] However, the JI mechanism was seen as developing towards a smoother and fairer arrangement.

Participation in the second commitment period was vigorously promoted in order to facilitate the continuation of JI. Despite the arguments that JI was insignificant to the Russian economy, its importance to companies implementing environmental regulations and improving their competitiveness by updating production technologies was emphasized. Cuts in the flaring of associated petroleum gas were taken as an example of the significant impacts that JI had generated in the Russian economy.[90]

Even though some project approvals were criticized as potentially corrupt and choice of project types seen to depart from the domestic guidelines established,[91] the environmental legitimacy of JI in Russia was never questioned directly. Thus, the benefits from JI projects seem to dominate this storyline. There were some synergies between this and the previous storyline dominated by the JI administration.

Developments of arguments, 2004–05 and 2010–12

The issue of control was an ongoing theme in the argument of the administration. Early on, caution was expressed against facilitating the JI scheme promoted by RAO UES Rossii. Later on, project owners and project developers were handpicked, and had to comply with requirements like having an office in Russia. The use of the revenues that companies received as a result of their JI projects was controlled by investment declaration, and Sberbank's role as a third party to JI contracts probably aimed at adding control too.

We can note several similarities between the early and implementation phase storylines. In both cases, the private sector – the beneficiaries of JI – argued for a longer implementation period, early JI in the case of 2004–05, and continuation of JI during the second commitment period in the 2010–12 debate. Also, 'losses' were reported, as criticism of the political leadership and administration. During the early period, these losses were linked to the projects which won tenders by foreign buyers but were not confirmed by the Russian government prior to adopting JI approval procedures. Later, they focused on decreasing prices of quotas while Russian projects awaited the adoption of the approval of the system, which took years for the domestic bureaucracy. Access to foreign emissions-trading schemes (mostly EU) was a topic of discussion during both periods. The electricity monopoly RAO UES Rossii was a particularly strong actor, but disappeared from the debate as a result of the liberalization of the Russian power market and the dismantling of this natural monopoly, whose facilities were auctioned off to private companies.

Recognition of the benefits to be gained from JI gradually developed when it became clear that such benefits were indeed real. This was no longer questioned in 2010–12, unlike earlier on when the total costs of projects – higher than expected revenues from quota sales – were cited as evidence of economically unfavourable deals for Russia. However, the discussion on demand for Russian quotas continued, mainly because the low participation in the pact made the question more acute. What seemed unchanged was the disagreement on the significance of JI revenues – state actors saw them as less significant than did the direct beneficiaries (companies), which kept arguing for the usefulness of these investments.

The importance of JI benefits was clearly not sufficient to push for participation in the Kyoto Protocol, but the importance of their role in pushing for ratification in 2004 can also be questioned. The main factors were obviously linked to foreign policy benefits.

There were fewer conspiracy theories in 2012, and those remaining were expressed in a more balanced way. However, the actions of the EU on climate policy (focusing on quotas from developing countries, support to the second commitment period) still seemed suspicious, and their environmental motivation somewhat questionable.

EMERGING DISCOURSES

From the above storylines, we can identify four main discourses that evolved concerning Russia's participation in the Kyoto Protocol, and more widely in the international climate regime.

Benefits Discourse

A recurrent theme in all four debates has been the benefits to be obtained by participating in the Kyoto regime. Actors in Russia have been very interested in the kinds of benefits available, how significant they are, and how to obtain them. No one in the domestic debate has questioned the legitimacy of benefits as a major driving factor for joining an environmental pact: Kyoto supporters as well as opponents have taken the benefits as a starting point for their argumentation. Typical benefit categories discussed have been economic benefits through the Kyoto mechanisms, image benefits through environmental actions, other foreign policy benefits and compensation for 'ecological services' provided by Russia's forests.

Supporters have seen a clear link between the investments available through the Kyoto mechanisms and Russian policy goals of modernizing industry and improving its energy efficiency. Even Putin's goal of doubling GDP, which was seen as obstructed by existing energy-intensity levels, was mentioned as one potential beneficiary. On the other hand, there were many voices demanding guarantees of such benefits against Russian ratification, often in terms of certainty of sufficient demand and price levels for Russian surplus allowances. Bringing the Kyoto regime into force was seen as a global contribution that merited compensation. This was also shown in President Putin's tactic of prolonging his decision on ratification; it seems highly likely that EU support to Russian WTO membership was the decisive benefit in the balance scale. This suggests that foreign policy was an important element in the process.

The focus on benefits completely ignores Russia's role as a major global emitter and the responsibility related to this. The rationale for accepting costly emissions-reduction burdens was absent because the security element related to the impacts of climate change passed almost unnoticed in the Russian debate. The whole regime seems to have been considered solely as a zero-sum game between the participants who divided the benefits: an economic rather than an environmental pact. This reflects the lack of understanding of the global environmental concerns that is the very rationale for negotiating climate agreements. Russia's crucial role in enabling the Kyoto Protocol to enter into force was even interpreted as an opportunity to demand more benefits in return. Further, certain elements of the pact were understood by some as 'promises' to particular countries, whereas in reality they were simply outcomes of various rules established during negotiations. Some opponents dismissed the benefits outlined by supporters as 'empty promises'.

The benefits discourse was clearly present also in debates on JI. The significance of investments was emphasized by proponents of JI and the Kyoto regime, whereas opponents considered the revenues from JI to be small in terms of the level of the Russian economy. This argument later on contributed to Russia's decision to drop out of the second period citing the low demand of and low price for Russian quotas.

The benefits-discourse also justified private sector arguments for launching JI early in order to obtain maximum benefits. Similarly, 'economic losses' were cited when blaming the government for inaction on enabling these benefits through JI. It was even suggested to establish a domestic emissions trading scheme, since in order to gain access to EU trading scheme – and its higher carbon prices – a domestic equivalent was required. However, the idea of launching a domestic trading scheme seems artificial, because such a policy instrument cannot function without an emissions cap strict enough to create a demand for reducing domestic emissions. Russia's loose Kyoto commitment allowed emissions growth – so no domestic policy instruments were required to facilitate emission reductions.

Open calls for benefits, especially guaranteed benefits, have gradually diminished. The argument that the benefits Russia receives will depend on Russia's own actions, especially those of the domestic administration, has grown stronger, adjusting Russian expectations towards a more realistic path.

Threats Discourse

The threats following from Russia's participation in Kyoto and its flexible mechanisms were debated as the counterforce to the benefits that could be obtained. Both opponents and supporters took part in this discourse, each trying to prove the other wrong.

Kyoto's main threat to Russia was considered to be the limitations to emissions growth, seen by many as directly linked to headroom for further economic growth. President Putin's goal of doubling the country's GDP was considered to be threatened by the Kyoto regime because Russia would have to limit its industrial activities in order to prevent emissions from overshooting its 1990 commitment level. Supporters saw this as highly unrealistic. The loss of industrial competitiveness in the global market was also noted as a related threat.

Various conspiracy theories were considered to contribute to the seriousness of the threats observed. Domestic interests in oversales of quotas, especially by the powerful oligarchs, were perceived as the main internal threat. Supporters of ratification and JI argued that state control over the quotas and their use would eliminate this threat. This approach was put in practice with JI – hand-picking eligible projects, requiring project owners to be registered as Russian companies, and controlling the use of revenues received through JI projects.

External threats were seen in 'sinister' motives among other Kyoto participants that would threaten Russian independence. Some saw Kyoto as a scheme for making Russia dependent on purchases of foreign technologies, or providing access to Russia's natural resources. Further, greater international oversight was feared as a result of emission control.

Threats were not considered against the threats posed by climate change, but rather against the correctness of the analysis of threats, and against the benefits available. The analysis of threats attracted considerable attention during the ratification debate, where presidential adviser Illarionov offered an extreme interpretation of Russia's future emission trends and the consequences of accepting commitments under the Kyoto pact. In the domestic debate, his arguments about the threats to Russia were widely seen as biased against the regime, as many experts argued the converse: that not much was required from Russia.

Over time, fewer threats were seen in using JI, perhaps as experience of the mechanism was gained, and attempts to make easy money through JI were rejected through state control. The desire to control domestic actors came up especially with JI; this was in order to avoid domestic private sector actors to gain control of the Russian carbon market. Perhaps JI was more attractive to the administration than emissions trading as it provided more opportunities for controlling market participants.[92] However, the same threat of emplacing limits on domestic economic growth by taking on further mitigation commitments remained an issue throughout the Kyoto second commitment period debate. As Russia's emissions grew during the first commitment period, and the envisaged target, 15–25 per cent reduction of the 1990 level, was becoming more challenging in comparison to the stabilization target of the first period, the caution had a firmer basis this time. The most radical conspiracy theories had disappeared by the end of the first commitment period, but distrust of the motives of other participants of the regime remained, gaining sophistication. Plotting against Russia as regards fair quota prices was mentioned, and even though the environmental motives behind EU climate policies were recognized, the perceived positive effects on technology imports as a result of international climate policy were still deemed suspect. Towards the end of the observation period, the Kyoto regime was for first time seen as a means to avoid a threat – EU 'carbon protectionism'.

Rationality Discourse

It has often been emphasized that the climate-sceptical views dominant in Russia's domestic climate debate are detrimental to adopting climate policies and to participation in international regimes in a meaningful manner. The discourse on the rationality of climate pacts such as Kyoto can explain much of the Russian background for such arguments.

The main scientific argument against the Kyoto regime concerned its inability to serve as a tool for solving the problem of climate change, that is, reducing atmospheric concentrations of greenhouse gases. This argument was more a matter of questioning the regime and its limited coverage and thus its inability to generate emissions reductions that would be sufficient to stop climate change, than the scientific validity of the theory of climate change. Russian claims that the regime 'lacks scientific basis' refer to this and may be misleading to Western audiences, whereas the Russians calling Kyoto 'inefficient' is likely to communicate the argument more clearly. This type of argumentation against the Protocol was considered as 'ecologically' based in Russia – again, somewhat different from the Western interpretation.

Arguments questioning the anthropogenic nature of climate change have in fact been presented in the Russian debate, although they have not had a dominant role in decision-making. Nevertheless, the negative nature of the net impacts of climate change on the Russian territory has been questioned, most famously by Putin himself. But rather than sheer climate scepticism – as often interpreted in the West – these arguments could be seen as representing the holism of the Russian approach to science in examining the problem. In contrast to the Western approach to the science of climate change as studied by the Intergovernmental Panel on Climate Change (IPCC), Russian actors tend to keep the options open for alternative interpretations and for the parallel effects of natural and anthropogenic climate changes[93] – most of which are also recognized by the IPCC itself, but have been less emphasized in Western debates. Also, changes to the environment are not automatically seen as solely detrimental: instead, analysis of positive and negative impacts, opportunities and challenges, is seen as the natural way of proceeding. All this can make the policy actions advocated by the Western consensus understanding seem potentially misguided and somewhat hysterical, rather than rational and scientific. It also leaves the door open for suspicions of deliberate over-interpretations – for instance by the EU in order to generate economic benefits – seen as explaining the rationality of such interpretations of some foreign participants.

Further argumentation against the rationality of the pact was related to the calculation of forest carbon sinks, based partly on political allocation rather than scientific estimates.[94] Here many Russian actors felt that the mere existence of Russia's forests merited 'ecological service' in the global scale, and even compensation. The Kyoto regime takes an activity-based approach – human-induced *changes* in land use and forestry, rather than its mere existence – to crediting carbon sinks.

Concerning scientific views, we should bear in mind that their relevance to decision-making depends greatly on the definition of the problem. If it is assumed that Russia's participation in international climate cooperation rests on concerns about the impacts of climate change, then the understanding of climate science is obviously decisive. However, we have seen that this is not the case, as other interests seem to drive decision-making. Therefore, stepping out of the Western environmental concerns-based discourse on climate change, scientific arguments on the validity of climate science should be seen as less crucial to policy action in the case of Russia than they first might seem.

Fairness Discourse

The final discourse identified focuses on the fairness of global climate cooperation, more specifically the Kyoto Protocol. It is interlinked with the rationality discourse: the main argument is that, since the above-explained lack of participation hampers the effectiveness of the regime, all countries should do their share to solve the problem. Even though Russia officially recognizes the principle of 'common but differentiated responsibilities' inscribed in the UN Framework Convention on Climate Change,[95] in reality, its negotiation position rejects the obligation of developed countries to act without the participation of the developing countries as an overriding principle. In practice, Russia (like several other countries) demands that the major emitters among the developing countries should take on commitments in order to bring together a sufficient share of the global greenhouse gas emissions to stop climate change, while rejecting unilateral demands on the developed countries only.

In the Russian view, Kyoto fails to provide sufficient coverage of global emissions. During the first commitment period when the industrialized countries were expected to take on commitments, the US dropped out and Canada withdrew later. The second commitment period was originally expected to widen the global coverage of the pact.[96] Instead, the circle of participating industrialized countries narrowed down even further, and none of the emerging economies took on commitments. As a result, Moscow has not considered it fair that Russia should have to take on commitments that would place limits on its economic development in the future, especially in comparison to the countries that reject commitments. The related Russian rhetoric has been that Kyoto is 'discriminatory' against Russia.

There are also other matters that are seen as 'fairness' issues. Russia feels that it has already exceeded its fair share in terms of reducing global emissions, as its emissions collapsed due to the closure of obsolete and redundant industrial production capacity in the aftermath of the Soviet Union. Other Kyoto participants have protested against this interpretation, seeing the emission collapse as a windfall rather than the result of genuine policy measures, as well as questioning how permanent the effect will be. Also, compensation for Russia's ecological services and bringing the Protocol into force has been seen as 'fair' by some. And finally, buyers have been blamed for price manipulation and 'discrimination' of Russian quotas in the carbon market, and the EU Emissions Trading Scheme[97] has been considered a 'fair' reference for Russian quota prices.

Geopolitics is obviously a strong undercurrent in this discourse. It seems even stronger as a driver of the policy process than economic benefits – benefits would have been concretely available from JI under the second commitment period, but the Russian leadership decided not to participate, based mainly on the Russian understanding of the global fairness of the pact. However, the implications of the difference of fairness interpretations of Russia and the international community as to image issues seem to drive Russia's policy process, at least in part. Even though it was argued that Russia can withdraw from Kyoto with a 'clear conscience' after the emission collapse and after having brought the Protocol into force, adopting a domestic emissions limitation target (September 2013) indicates that Moscow has remained aware of its image in terms of global fairness of participation in efforts aimed at mitigating the effects of climate change. The domestic target is probably seen as replacing an international commitment to some extent.

Also the interpretations of fairness have shifted over time. While the main argument that all major emitters should take commitments remains unchanged, in 2012 President Medvedev declared that it was only fair that Russia was not receiving any significant benefits from JI as its domestic administrative performance had been so poor. This represents a major shift in the interpretation of 'fairness' in the Kyoto regime, with Russia recognizing its own role in what it gains, rather than seeing fairness as a generally acceptable justification for a position regardless of the validity of the argument itself.

CONCLUSIONS

This chapter has sought to identify dominant discourses in Russia, and assess their role in domestic policy and position formation. In Russian climate policy, foreign policy interests clearly drive decision-making. Such elements featured especially in the rationality and fairness discourses, while the threats discourse focused more on economic losses. The benefits discourse included both foreign policy benefits and economic benefits. In the debate on ratification of the Kyoto Protocol, discourses opposing it seemed stronger in the domestic debate, but the benefits as regards foreign policy proved decisive in the end. By contrast, when the benefits boiled down to private sector economic benefits – however strongly expressed in the domestic discourse – the Kyoto second commitment period was rejected on the basis of foreign policy argumentations related to fairness and rationality discourses. The JI debate was dominated by the benefit discourse. Initially, the threats discourse, and the overly-emphasized need for state control that followed, contributed to the long delay in establishing the domestic administration for JI. Further down the line, the benefits of JI, albeit increasingly vocally argued by JI beneficiaries and already proven by experience, were overridden. The threat discourse and especially the foreign policy-focused fairness and rationality discourses dominated in the presidential administration, with the emphasis on the geopolitical big picture of the climate regime. Thus, state policies seldom seem to follow the domestic discourses in the sense of the dominant discourse directing Russia's position on the international level. The main contradiction was between the heavy emphasis on the benefits Russia could gain from the regime in the domestic debates, and the foreign policy interests as outlined by the presidential administration and its close circle.

Regardless, discourses by the domestic actors help to outline the national starting points for a policy debate. They also provide a glimpse behind the scenes of the national policy rhetoric used at the international level, and explain the underlying assumptions. With climate matters, grasping this connection has been difficult for Russia's Western negotiation counterparts. Here a comparison of the Russian climate discourses with the fundamental elements of the climate regime as inscribed in the UN climate pacts can facilitate better understanding. The principles and aims of the UN Framework Convention on Climate Change (the Convention) and the Kyoto Protocol are taken as a starting point, and the Russian position is compared to this and put in the context of the positions of other major players.

The definition of the *necessity to act* to prevent climate change is linked to the 'precautionary principle'. According to the Convention, 'where there are threats of serious or irreversible damage, lack of full scientific certainty should not be used as a reason for postponing such measures'. This principle is well recognized in the climate negotiations. Most countries agree; however, national interests, especially economic ones, are often prioritized over environmental concerns, even though these concerns may have been genuine and a major driver behind the country's participation.

Our analysis has shown that this does not apply to Russia. Environmental concerns are of course officially recognized as a reason for participating – but are almost completely absent as a supporting argument in the domestic debate. Domestic actors seem to agree that if Russia cannot expect to receive any benefits from participation, non-participation is justifiable. Thus, the real environment-related driver for Russia emerges as environmental concerns on the part of other governments, and the resultant opportunities for being compensated for participation. Global cooperation against climate change is commonly considered as a positive-sum game because of the collective gains from avoiding the impacts of global climate change. However, when the impacts of climate change are *not* a genuine concern that features in the equation of the Russian decision-makers, the whole picture becomes more of a zero-sum game.

Some countries receive benefits and exemptions, while others must on take burdens. Russia is not the only, or even the most famous, party to adopt elements of this approach; in practice, in rejecting the Kyoto Protocol, the US stated that its impact would be too heavy on the national economy.

The *division of responsibilities* in climate action is defined by the Convention as follows: 'the largest share of historical and current global emissions of greenhouse gases has originated in developed countries'. What follows is that 'the developed country Parties should take the lead in combating climate change and the adverse effects'. This division of historical responsibilities was more clear-cut at the time when the Convention and the Kyoto Protocol were negotiated. Since then, the developing country group has further diversified, as some countries have succeeded in developing their economies and achieving greater prosperity. As a result, this principle has turned into a fundamental disagreement between parties: it was the main reason which led to the failure of the regime in terms of global coverage when first the US and Canada, and then also other industrialized countries opted out, as a result of the lack of commitments by the major emitting emerging economies of China and India. Even though the consensus, as a starting point of the agreement, was that the developed countries which have caused the problem should take the lead, the prevailing philosophy in industrialized countries has shifted to bringing together a critical mass of global emissions which cannot be achieved without China and India. This is, of course, opposed by many of the developing countries, which want to retain their privilege. In this sense, Russia's fairness and rationality discourses that all major emitters must take commitments to achieve the critical mass required for solving the problem – and that it is not fair to require developed countries to act unless the large emerging economies also join in – is close to the current mainstream stance of the group of industrialized countries in the climate negotiations.

Views are more divided as to *the role of Russia as a transition economy*. Both the Convention and Kyoto recognize that 'in the implementation of their commitments . . . a certain degree of flexibility shall be allowed . . . to the Parties included in Annex I undergoing the process of transition to a market economy, in order to enhance the ability of these Parties to address climate change'. However, due to its loose target that allowed emission growths during the first commitment period, Russia has often been seen as a free-rider as regards emissions-reduction measures. The post-Soviet emissions collapse is not accepted as an emissions-reduction measure by other parties and Russia is not seen as acting in line with its level of historical responsibility. Its special status as a transition economy is no longer taken as sufficient justification for non-action by most other parties. The Russian understanding is that Russia has done its fair share and more, as the decline in its emissions represents a significant share of total global emission reductions in comparison to 1990 levels. Further, Russia expects to receive future benefits in return for its environmentally favourable performance, such as participation in a climate regime. This is sheer bargaining, as Russia has some weight to throw around in negotiations.

All this demonstrates how different logics can lead to differing rationalities in terms of policy positions. However, after familiarizing ourselves with the discourses underlying Russia's position, these statements about the Russian approach should seem more logical. From the discourses, we have a better idea of what the positions are based on. But what do we learn from the Russian discourses on climate change concerning the main question of this book? Can the motivations behind Russia's approach to climate policy be reduced to motivations directly related or unrelated to environmental concern? One could interpret the findings as the latter: the evidence indicates that motivations for participating are related to issues other than trying to solve the problem of climate change as such. In terms of benefits, foreign policy gains seem to be decisive, and economic benefits are considered as a plus.

One of the key conclusions based on the discourses presented above – and a fundamental difference between the Western and Russian climate discourses – is that environmental benefits from climate mitigation *per se*, as understood in the West and outlined above, have not been recognized in the Russian debate. Instead, they have been considered in terms of the interests of other participants of the regime, thus playing along with them. However, Russian decision-making centres on the total impact of the Kyoto regime to the carbon concentration of the atmosphere and the related fairness discourse: responsibility to participate is seen to emerge only when the total action reaches the critical mass sufficient to limit or stop climate change. Further, the rationality discourse opposes action for political reasons (common but differentiated responsibilities) if there is no chance of solving the problem through that action. In these terms, the 'inefficiency' or 'lack of scientific basis' argumentation against Kyoto was environmental – or 'ecological', to use the Russian term.

That said, it cannot be ignored that given the current deadlock of the UN climate negotiations, the fairness and rationality discourses conveniently lead to justification of non-action. Also, there is currently no major conflict between the fairness discourse, which seems to recognize that climate change should be stopped if participation reaches a level that makes a real impact physically possible, and the rationality discourse which de facto rejects the precautionary principle by requiring scientific certainty to justify action. A real test of which discourse is the strongest – and whether what is called 'ecological' really covers environmental concerns – would be a situation in which others were ready to cooperate, leaving Russia to decide whether to be 'in' or 'out'. Even then, we should exclude the possibility of foreign policy interests as the main driver behind such a decision.

NOTES

1. Annex I originally consisted of what is now the EU-27, the US, Canada, Japan, Australia, New Zealand, Switzerland, Norway, Russia and Ukraine. The US did not ratify the pact initially; Canada withdrew from it in 2011; and Russia, Japan and New Zealand rejected further commitments under the second Kyoto Protocol period. Belarus and Kazakhstan launched processes to join Annex I and Annex B, but were too late to join the first commitment period.
2. Data from: http://mdgs.un.org/unsd/mdg/SeriesDetail.aspx?srid=749&crid= (accessed 14 September 2014).
3. Source: author's calculations, based on data available at: http://unfccc.int/di/DetailedByParty.do (accessed 14 September 2014).
4. There were concerns that, if Russian emissions recovered to the pre-Soviet collapse level along with the GDP, Russia might end up emitting the amount allowed by its quotas. The country was not implementing any focused emissions-reduction policies or measures, because the loose Kyoto target did not offer incentives for such activities; therefore, increasing emissions during the first commitment period could have led to Russia needing its already sold quotas. In practice, the country would have ended up in non-compliance, and the quotas sold to other countries could have become nullified in terms of their environmentally regulative impact.
5. Although fairly precise rules for implementation had been agreed in Marrakech in 2001, prior to Russia's ratification, many questions remained.
6. *Kommersant*, 23 October 2004: 'Duma vybrala Kioto' (Дума выбрала Киото).
7. *Open Economy*, 9 September 2004: 'Fradkov kritikuet Kiotskii protokol. V pisme Putiny on nazivaet protokol neeffektivnoi, nespravedlivoi i nevygodnoi initsiativoi', available at: www.opec.ru/1055626.html (accessed 24 July 2013).
8. *Rosbalt*, 8 September 2003: 'Ratifikatsiia Kiotskogo protokola ne pomeshaet Rossii udvoit VVP', available: at www.rosbalt.ru/main/2003/09/08/117494.html (accessed 4 June 2003).
9. *Open Economy*, 9 September 2004.
10. V. Gratchev, presentation in the State Duma, and V. Zubov, Deputy from Edinnaya Rossia Party, statement during the ratification debate, 22 October 2004. Duma transcript, available through: http://transcript.duma.gov.ru/ (accessed 14 September 2014) (see further, Statement in the State Duma). *InoCMI.ru*, 18 May 2004: 'V rukah Rossii 'zhizn i smert' Kiotskogo dogovora', available at: http://inosmi.ru/inrussia/20040518/209673.html (accessed 24 July 2013).
11. I. Bashmakov, 'Rossiia i ratifikatsiia Kiotskogo protokola', available at: www.cenef.ru/file/Bpaper104.pdf (accessed 14 September 2014). Year of publication not indicated.
12. V. Zubov, Deputy from Edinnaya Rossia Party, statement in the State Duma.
13. V. Gratchev, speech in the State Duma.
14. *Rosbalt*, 10 April 2003: 'Rossiia poteriaet zarubezhnyh stran, esli ne podnishet Kiotskii protokol, schitaiut v Minenergo RF', available at: www.rosbalt.ru/main/2003/04/10/93301.html (accessed 8 May 2014). V. Gratchev, speech in the State Duma.
15. *Open Economy*, 18 May 2004: 'Ekspertnye mneniia: Minpromenergo i RAN pazoshlis v rekomendatsiiah Putinu po Kiotskomu protokolu', available at: www.opec.ru/news_doc.asp?d_no=48375 (accessed 16 June 2013). A. Bedritsky, speech in the State Duma, 22 October 2004.
16. See for instance *Novaya Gazeta*, 8 July 2009: 'Kiotskii protokol'. Commentary by

Danilov-Danylian, available at: www.novayagazeta.ru/politics/44425.html (accessed 26 July 2013).

17. S. Eduardov, 'Kioto stanet dlia Rossii novoi Tsusimoi', *Utro.ru*, 24 September 2004, available at: www.utro.ru/articles/2004/09/24/354159.shtml (accessed 8 May 2014).
18. A. Bedritsky, speech in the State Duma.
19. The main document presenting this view was Institut ekonomichskogo analiza (2003). See also Yu. Izrael and P. Romanov of the Communist Party, statements in the State Duma.
20. Izrael and Romanov (note 19 above).
21. *InoCMI.ru*, 18 May 2004.
22. N. Olefirenko, in the radio debate organized by *Radio Svoboda* 6 October 2003. Script available at: http://archive.svoboda.org/programs/eco/2003/eco.100603.asp (accessed 24 July 2013).
23. *Rosbalt*, 21 March 2003: 'Ratifikatsiia Kiotskogo protokola dliia Rossii ne imeet ekonomitseskogo ili ekologitseskogo smysla, stsitaet zamestitel glavy Minekonomrazvitiia', available at: www.rosbalt.ru/main/2003/03/21/90223.html. *RBK Daily*, 20 May 2004: 'Kiotskii protokol ne nuzen Rossii', available at: www.rbcdaily.ru/industry/562949979065872 (accessed 4 June 2013). Eduardov (note 17 above).
24. A. Ostrovsky (Liberal-Democratic Party LDPR), statement in the State Duma.
25. Institut ekonomichskogo analiza (2003).
26. *InoCMI.ru*, 18 May 2004.
27. Ostrovsky (note 24 above).
28. *Rosbalt*, 7 May 2003: 'Kiotskii protokol sushchestvenno ne zamedlit tempov global-nogo potepleniia, stsitaet direktor Institute globalnogo klimata i ekologii Yuri Izrael', available at: www.rosbalt.ru/main/2003/05/07/97196.html (accessed 8 May 2014). *Open Economy*, 18 May 2004: 'Ekspertnye mneniia: Minpromenergo i RAN pazoshlis v reko-mendatsiiah Putinu po Kiotskomu protokolu', available at: www.opec.ru/news_doc.asp?d_no=48375 (accessed 16 June 2013).
29. N. Narotsnitskaya of the Rodina Party, statement in the State Duma.
30. Ostrovsky (note 24 above).
31. Narotsnitskaya (note 29 above).
32. Ibid.
33. A. Ostrovsky (Liberal-Democratic party LDPR), statement in the State Duma.
34. O. Proskurnaya and A. Bekker, 'Rossiia protiv gazov', *Vedomosti*, 30 September 2004. *Rosbalt*, 7 May 2003.
35. *Ria Novosti*, 10 February 2004: 'Gordeev: Kiotskii Protokol ne ulushchit ekologiiu'.
36. *Rosbalt*, 4 June 2003: 'Andrei Illarionov: preimushchestva ratifikatsii Kiotskogo protokola dliia Rossii dostatochno prizrachny', available at: www.rosbalt.ru/main/2003/06/04/101730.html
37. *Open Economy*, 18 May 2004.
38. *InoCMI.ru*, 18 May 2004.
39. *Open Economy*, 18 May 2004.
40. *Rosbalt*, 8 July 2004: 'Illarionov: Kiotskii protokol – novaia forma totalitarnogo rezhima', available at: www.rosbalt.ru/main/2004/07/08/169526.html (accessed 2 June 2013).
41. *Polit.ru*, 18 May 2004: 'Kiotskii protokol: Akademiia nauk pomogla Putinu', available at: http://polit.ru/article/2004/05/18/kyoto/ (accessed 24 July 2013). *InoCMI.ru*, 18 May 2004. *RIA Novosti*, 13 May 2004: 'Ratifikatsiia kiotskogo protokola stala politicheskim voprosom v otnosheniia Rossii i Evrosoiuzam – ekspert'.
42. *Rosbalt*, 4 June 2003: 'Andrei Illarionov: preimushchestva ratifikatsii Kiotskogo protokola dliia Rossii dostatochno prizrachny', available at: www.rosbalt.ru/main/2003/06/04/101730.html (accessed 14 November 2011).
43. E. Lyubarskaya, 'Pravitelstvo ne znaet, zachem odobrilo Kiotskii protokol', *Lenta.ru*, 1 October 2004, available at: http://lenta.ru/articles/2004/09/30/kioto/ (accessed 4 June 2013).

44. V. Potapov, 'Protokolnie torgi',. *Rossiskaya Gazeta*, 15 April 2004. *RIA Novosti*, 13 May 2004.
45. Potapov (note 44 above).
46. D. Ten Kate and A. Morales, 'Japan, Russia Won't Take on New Kyoto Targets, UN's Climate Chief Says', *Bloomberg*, 8 April 2011, available at: www.bloomberg.com/news/2011-04-08/no-nation-fundamentally-opposes-extending-kyoto-treaty-un-s-figueres-says.html (accessed 24 July 2013).
47. S. Kulikov, 'Rossiia ostaetsia v Kiotskom protokolec chistoi sovestiu', *Nezavizimaya Gazeta*, 11 December 2012.
48. A. Shapovalov, 'Kiotskii vopros reshat sovetniki prezidenta', *Kommersant*, 15 October 2012.
49. O. Samofalova, 'Ruchkoi pomashem Kiotskomu protokolu', *Vzglyad*, 18 October 2012.
50. M. Lyotova, 'Vozduhom ne torguem', *Vedomosti*, 26 November 2012. *Neft Rossii*, 6 August 2010: 'Konflikt interesov'.
51. M. Dovgyallo, 'Zakat nadnatsionalnyh kvot', *HG-Energya*, 11 December 2012.
52. A. Galenovich, 'Riski i vozmozhnosti regulirovaniia parnikovyh vybrosov', *NG-Energiia*, 19 June 2012.
53. A. Shapovalov and A. Davydova, 'Klimaticheskoe bessoznatelnoe', *Kommersant*, 7 December 2012.
54. A.Shapovalov, 'Iskopaemoe vchrashnego dnia', *Kommersant*, 30 November 2012.
55. S. Kulikov, 'Rossiia ostaetsia v Kiotskom protokolec chistoi sovestiu', *Nezavizimaya Gazeta*, 11 December 2012.
56. A. Shapovalov and A. Davydova, 'Klimaticheskoe bessoznatelnoe', *Kommersant*, 7 December 2012.
57. *Nezavizimaya Gazeta*, 26 November 2012: 'Ot redaktsii'.
58. A. Shapovalov, 'Moskva zabludilas v Kioto-2', *Kommersant*, 22 November 2012.
59. A. Shapovalov, 'Kiotskii vopros reshat sovetniki prezidenta', *Kommersant*, 15 October 2012.
60. Shapovalov (note 58 above).
61. Shapovalov (note 59 above).
62. A. Shapovalov, 'Ekologicheski chistyi biznes', *Kommersant*, 5 March 2004.
63. *Ria Novosti*, 19 May 2004: 'Upushchennaia vygoda RAO EES ot neratifikatsii Rossiei Kiotsogo Protokola za dva goda sostavila okolo 60 mln evro'.
64. *Kommersant*, 1 April 2005: 'Chnovniki ne toroviatsia v Kioto'.
65. *Vedomosti*, 14 January 2005: 'Rossiiskie kompanii ne mogut torgovat kvotami ha vybros gazov'.
66. I. Rybaltsenko and A. Shapovalov, 'RAO "EES Rossii" nachnet dengi iz vozduha', *Kommersant*, 28 June 2005.
67. A. Shapovalov, 'Protokol pazdora', *Kommersant*, 15 April 2004.
68. State Duma ratification discussion, 22 October 2004. Duma transcript, available at: http://transcript.duma.gov.ru/ (accessed 14 September 2014).
69. *Vedomosti*, 14 January 2005.
70. A. Gratchev, presentation in the State Duma.
71. A. Shapovalov, 'Uglekiclyi rynok', *Kommersant*, 22 October 2004.
72. *Kommersant*, 23 October 2004: 'Duma vybrala Kioto Protokol'.
73. N. Narotsnitskaya (Rodina Party), statement in the State Duma.
74. *Rosbalt*, 7 May 2003: 'Kiotskii protokol sushchestvenno ne zamedlit tempov global-nogo potepleniia, stsitaet direktor Institute globalnogo klimata i ekologii Yuri Izrael', available at: www.rosbalt.ru/main/2003/05/07/97196.html (accessed 8 May 2014). *Open Economy*, 18 May 2004: 'Ekspertnye mneniia: Minpromenergo i RAN pazoshlis v reko-mendatsiiah Putinu po Kiotskomu protokolu', available at: www.opec.ru/news_doc.asp?d_no=48375 (accessed 16 June 2013).
75. *PointCarbon*, 26 July 2011: 'Russian President wants JI approvals without tenders'.
76. 'It must be admitted that no particular benefits were received from the Kyoto Protocol in terms of a commercial plan, we did not manage to take advantage [of the Kyoto

221

22211312122112

Protocol] – and that is absolutely fair': in O. Samofalova, 'Ruchkoi pomashem Kiotskomu protokolu', *Vzglyad*, 18 October 2012.

77. *Ria Novosti*, 28 July 2010: 'WWF: priniatie "kiotskih" projektov priblizhaet otkaz ot szhiganiia gaza'.

78. A. Shapovalov, 'Kiotskii vopros reshat sovetniki prezidenta', *Kommersant*, 15 October 2012.

79. *IA Marimedia*, 19 August 2011: 'Modernizatsiia tehnologichskih protsessov v Rossii proshla za schet rossiiskih investitsii'.

80. *Ria Novosti*, 25 May 2011: 'Minprirody i SB obsydit ispolzovanie sredstv "kiotskie" proektov'.

81. *PointCarbon*, 25 November 2009: 'Russia's new JI rules could break logjam'.

82. The true-up period is the time during which Annex I industrialized country groups can calculate their emissions and sinks, and quotas acquired from foreign sources, in order to check how close they are to their target adopted under the first commitment period. This period allows them then to achieve compliance status by purchasing/selling in order to even out any deficit/surplus.

83. *Ria Novosti*, 4 April 2011: 'Kiotskii mehanizm v Rossii: odin god, dva konkursa, 33 proektov'.

84. Lyotova 2012 (note 50 above).

85. *PointCarbon*, 17 August 2011: 'Sberbank sees weak demand at carbon tender'.

86. M. Dovgyallo, 'Zakat nadnatsionalnyh kvot', *HG-Energiia* 11 December 2012. A. Shapovalov, 'Minekonomiki pooasnilo pravila igry na "kiotskom" rynke', *Kommersant*, 24 January 2011.

87. Y. Kravtsenko, 'Milliard na vozduhe', *Vedomosti*, 28 April 2009.

88. A. Shovalov, A. Davydova and D. Butrin, Dmitry, 'Sberbank boretsia sytechkami ygleroga', *Kommersant*, 24 December 2010. M. Yulkin and K. Zabelin, 'Proekti sovmestnogo osushchestvleniia v Rossii' (po sostoianiiu na 23 oktobria 2012 goda). Analytical note, OOO «CCGS».

89. M. Yulkin, 'Kiotskie mehanizmy v Rossii snova zabuksovali', unpublished draft circulated by the author in 2010. *PointCarbon*, 29 June 2011: 'Russian business group produces JI wish list'.

90. *Ria Novosti*, 28 July 2010: 'WWF: priniatie "kiotskih" projektov priblizhaet otkaz ot szhiganiia gaza'. *Neft Rossii*, 6 August 2010: 'Konflikt interesov'.

91. O. Senova, 'Rossiia snova meniaet pravila igry po Kiotskom proektam – stavit novye barery dlia nizkouglerodnoi ekonomiki', *Rossiiskoi sotsialno-ekologicheskii soius*, 30 September 2011. O. Podosenova, 'Kiotskie proekti Sberbanka – otrasli na vybros?', *Rossiiskoi sotsialno-ekologicheskii soius*, 28 August 2011.

92. However, the fact that Russia never engaged in emissions trading was due mainly to the lack of demand for assigned amount units (AAUs) once Russia would finally be ready to sell.

93. The parallel effects are also recognized by the Inter-Governmental Panel on Climate Change but have not been emphasized by Western media and policy-makers.

94. Due mainly to the lack of scientific understanding of various types of carbon sinks, as well as the lack of consensus on calculation methodologies.

95. UN Framework Convention on Climate Change, Art. 3: The Parties should protect the climate system for the benefit of present and future generations of humankind, on the basis of equity and in accordance with their common but differentiated responsibilities and respective capabilities. Accordingly, the developed country Parties should take the lead in combating climate change and the adverse effects thereof.

96. Several prosperous countries – among them, South Korea, Singapore and Qatar – are still categorized as developing countries, and thus escape any binding commitments.

97. EU Emissions Trading Scheme has its internal market, and is thus price-dependent on internal demand – which was higher than the international prices for some time.

4. The regional case: protecting the environment of the Baltic Sea

INTRODUCTION

The Baltic Sea is regarded as one of the most polluted sea areas in the world (HELCOM 2007). The Helsinki Convention on the Protection of the Marine Environment of the Baltic Sea area, agreed upon in 1974, was the first international agreement to cover an entire sea. With its governing body the Helsinki Commission (HELCOM), the Convention forms an environmental protection regime that includes all the Baltic coastal countries. Even if the impact of the HELCOM regime on the state of the environment has been rather modest as yet (see Artioli et al. 2008), the regime stands as one of the most active cases of regional environmental cooperation, offering lessons for scholars and practitioners of international environmental politics (see e.g. Haas 1993; VanDeveer 2004; Tynkkynen 2011).

According to the HELCOM Baltic Sea Action Plan (BSAP) (see HELCOM 2007), the most serious environmental problem in the Baltic Sea is eutrophication: the accumulation of excessive nutrients, mainly phosphorus and nitrogen, in the water, with subsequent accelerated primary production leading to toxic algal blooms (cyanobacteria), oxygen depletion, and biodiversity loss. These effects have a negative influence on recreational activities, tourism and fishery, and even human health. Nutrients originate mainly from anthropogenic sources throughout the drainage basin: (urban) wastewater, industrial and agricultural activities, forestry, and transport. In addition to eutrophication, the input of hazardous substances, biodiversity loss and growing maritime activities, such as oil transport, have been identified as problems for the Baltic Sea environment. The ecology of the Baltic Sea is particularly sensitive because of certain hydrographic and geochemical characteristics, including a large drainage basin, long renewal times, strong stratification and variable bottom topography. In addition, the varying societal histories and non-simultaneous socio-economic development of the Baltic Sea coastal countries have made environmental governance of the sea an intricate task (see Tynkkynen 2013; Pihlajamäki and Tynkkynen 2011b). Russia is one of the most important single actors in the Baltic Sea region. It has committed itself to the Baltic Sea environmental cooperation: it is a signatory to the Helsinki Convention and participates in the activities of HELCOM. In 2007, Russia signed the BSAP, which now shapes the activities of coastal countries within the HELCOM regime.

This chapter examines Russia's participation in the HELCOM regime since the early 1970s.[1] It describes the formation and the evolution of the regime in general and introduces the main storylines which summarize various Russian narratives on Baltic Sea environmental cooperation at different times. Prior to the concluding section, the discourses emerging from the storylines are sketched.

BACKGROUND

Russia and the Baltic Sea

Russia exerts significant influence on the environmental state of the Baltic Sea, despite having only two per cent of the total catchment area. According to HELCOM (2009: p.77), Russia ranks second of the Baltic Sea coastal countries in total emissions of phosphorous and third in nitrogen emissions. The Russian coasts of the Baltic Sea, the Gulf of Finland in particular, have long been recognized as 'pockets of point and non-point source contaminants' (see Feldman and Blokov 2012, p.27). This pollution originates mainly from the major Russian cities in the catchment area: St Petersburg, Kaliningrad, Pskov and Petrozavodsk. The negative impact of the city of St Petersburg on the Baltic Sea has lessened alongside the modernization of the water sector (for example, the construction of the South West wastewater treatment plant and the main sewage collector) and the introduction of chemical phosphorus removal in wastewater treatment plants. However, effluents generated from industry, in addition to increased transport, continue to generate large volumes of water pollution, such as heavy metals and phenols, in St Petersburg and the Leningrad regions (see Trumbull 2007). Especially in the Leningrad region, agricultural runoff poses a growing threat, because the number of large farms is increasing; the Russian government has declared the goal of increasing chicken and egg production in the Leningrad region considerably within the next few years.[2]

Also in the Kaliningrad region the waterways are highly polluted. Pollution in the Pregol River and Primorsk Bay is ten times above the levels stipulated by HELCOM, and 20 times higher than EU standards,[3] and concentrations of phenol and oil in Pionerskii and Baltiskii port areas are five to ten times higher than normal (see Korotkova 2008). The lack of a modern wastewater treatment system throughout the Kaliningrad region is a major deficiency: according to the *Federal Target Programme for the Development of the Kaliningrad Region until 2015*, less than 10 per cent of the towns and villages of the region are equipped with biological sewage treatment systems.[4] Another serious problem is vessel-source pollution of sea waters and coastal zones (Nechiporuk and Nozhenko 2010, p. 110).

According to Feldman and Blokov (2012, p. 27), water pollution problems in Russia have in recent years shifted from industrial discharges and agricultural runoff to municipal wastewater discharges, which accounted for some two-thirds of water pollutants in 2005. This is reflected also in the coverage of the central and regional press in Russia: between 2006 and 2013, about 75 per cent of all news stories related to the Baltic Sea discussed municipal wastewater treatment.[5] Another issue regularly taken up in connection with the Baltic Sea environment has been energy transport; especially in 2006 and 2007, the potential environmental threats posed by the construction of the Nord Stream gas pipeline attracted considerable publicity in Russia, and also later there was much discussion of the environmental safety of new ports and other energy infrastructure.

Russia does not have a specific domestic Baltic Sea environmental policy, except for recent national level programmes (see below). The Baltic Sea environment is low on the list of political priorities, and public awareness is modest. Due to the complex and constantly changing structure of Russian environmental administration, and given that, in principle, it is the federal government that signs and ratifies international documents that regulate Russia's responsibility in protecting the Baltic Sea, it is often unclear which body has responsibility for ensuring the implementation of HELCOM provisions.[6] Certain recommendations are implemented through federal regulation (in the Water Code,[7] for example, or in the planned Russian version of the water framework directive) – but in terms of regional strategies and implementation, the unclear division of labour obstructs action. In principle, competencies of the state environmental control lie at the regional level since the 2004 reform of the federal structure of the Russian Federation, but in some regions it has taken several years to create the necessary institutions. For example, in the Kaliningrad region the Service for Environmental Control and Supervision began operations only in 2009 (Nechiporuk et al. 2011, pp. 47–8). Moreover, water pollution intersects with many administrative branches and sectors, making the division and sharing of responsibilities even more intricate. It is difficult to say to what extent the various HELCOM provisions and recommendations have been implemented in Russia – or, more accurately, whether certain regulative measures have been taken because of HELCOM, or for other reasons.

The main actors that engage in the protection of the Baltic Sea in Russia can roughly be divided into two: those experts and officials who participate in the work of HELCOM and those, mainly non-governmental organizations and local actors, who exercise practical cooperation with foreign partners in the framework of HELCOM. The most important actor in the first group is a private expert organization called Ekologia i Biznes [Ecology and Business], which forms the practical link between HELCOM and domestic actors. In practice, there is one man, Mr Leonid Korovin, 'Mr Russian HELCOM', who represents Russia in HELCOM. He also seems to have been the main author of the Russian National Implementation Programme of the BSAP.[8] Basically, he coordinates all interaction between Russia and HELCOM.[9]

In the early 1990s, certain local actors, such as the water and sewage utility of St Petersburg, managed to take advantage of the administrative turbulence and establish their own contacts across the border (see Tynkkynen 2008b), and have maintained these contacts since then. There are also several non-governmental organizations (NGOs) very active in Baltic Sea issues. Perhaps the best known of these is Ecodefense in Kaliningrad, which in 2007 received the Swedish Baltic Sea Water Award for its efforts to raise awareness of the Baltic Sea environment.[10] In addition, there are other NGOs, such as the Friends of the Baltic, Baltic Fund for Nature of St Petersburg Naturalists' Society and Greenpeace (St Petersburg and Leningrad oblast), with the Baltic Sea environment on their agendas. The main focus of most these NGOs is on educational activities and raising environmental awareness among schoolchildren[11] (see also Tynkkynen 2006), which also backs up the activities of the HELCOM regime.

THE HELCOM REGIME

The Helsinki Convention on the Protection of the Marine Environment of the Baltic Sea Area was both a follow-up to the UN Conference on the Human Environment held in Stockholm in 1972, and a reaction to the growing scientific concerns over the health of the Baltic Sea (Darst 2001, p. 53; Brusendorff 2006, p. 64). Signed by all the (then) seven littoral Baltic Sea countries in 1974,[12] the Convention was the first international agreement to cover an entire sea – including all sources of pollution from land, ships, oil and chemical spills, airborne pollutants, offshore dumping, and seabed exploitation (HELCOM 1993).

The Convention was also pioneering in that it was the first multilateral environmental agreement between members of two competing military alliances. Of the seven signatories, three (the USSR, Poland and the German Democratic Republic) were members of the Warsaw Pact and two (the Federal Republic of Germany and Denmark) belonged to the North Atlantic Treaty Organization (NATO); Finland and Sweden were considered politically neutral (Räsänen and Laakkonen 2008, p. 44). Peter Ehlers, who served as HELCOM Chairman from 1984–86 and 2000–02, has praised the political significance of the Convention by noting that:

> the protection of the Baltic Sea was one of the very first issues which the Baltic Sea States agreed to cooperate on. It can justifiably be said that wide-ranging co-operation within the bodies of the Helsinki Commission, established by the convention in 1974, and the personal contacts made through this work all led to improved understanding, greater openness and mutual understanding. In a modest way, this helped to overcome the split of the world into East and West, and later to tear down the Iron Curtain. (HELCOM 2004a, p. 6)

Because of the economic and political concerns of the Soviet leadership, including the fear of external interference in internal affairs, and military-industrial intelligence of the West, coastal waters were in practice exempted from the Convention: it was agreed that 'each Contracting Party shall implement the provisions of the present convention within its territorial sea through its national authorities' (HELCOM 1989, p. 3; see also Haas 1993, p. 143; VanDeveer 2011, p. 40). The USSR claimed its territorial waters to be defined in the Convention up to 12 miles from its coast, and the other coastal states echoed this. In certain ecologically critical, narrow areas such as the Gulf of Finland, this meant total exclusion from the purview of the Convention (Darst 2001, p. 58). In addition, the internal waters of member states were excluded from the Convention, even though riverborne pollutants accounted for well over half the land-based pollution load to the Baltic Sea.

The first decade of HELCOM's work was dedicated to creating a common understanding about the environmental problems of the sea and how to measure the pollution loads entering the sea from land-based activities (Brusendorff 2006, p. 65). Following from the scientific focus, the first impact of the existence of HELCOM on East-West interaction was greater specialist cooperation (Darst 2001, pp. 53–4). Thereby, participation in HELCOM had a significant impact on the development of Baltic marine science in the Soviet Union. The first practical measures within the regime were taken in the 1970s to restrict the use of certain hazardous substances. One of these decisions concerned phasing out the use of polychlorinated biphenyls (PCBs), which had proven primarily responsible for, *inter alia*, the serious decline in the white-tailed eagle population of the Baltic Sea area (Brusendorff 2006, p. 65). Also addressed from the very beginning were the negative environmental impacts of shipping, a topic chosen mainly in order to influence new international shipping regulations and ensure their harmonized implementation in the region (ibid.).

Eutrophication gradually came to feature on the list of Baltic Sea environmental problems (see assessments in HELCOM 1980; 1987; 1996). It was not until the second half of the 1980s that HELCOM adopted the first recommendations for limiting nutrient pollution from municipal waste-water treatment plants, agriculture and industry. In 1988, a Ministerial Declaration on the Protection of the Marine Environment of the Baltic Sea Area was adopted by the ministers responsible for environmental protection in the Baltic Sea states. It set the target of reducing discharges of heavy metals and toxic or persistent organic substances and nutrients by 50 per cent 'as soon as possible but not later than 1995' (HELCOM 1988). This target was never reached – but, as scholars have argued, the importance of the Ministerial Declaration lay more in its demonstration of the political will to take practical steps, than in its direct environmental outcomes (see Hiltunen 1994; Hjort 1996).

The dissolution of the USSR and the collapse of the state socialist bloc put an end to Baltic Sea environmental cooperation in its early form. In 1992, the new Helsinki Convention was signed by all states bordering on the Baltic Sea, and by the European Community[13] (see Figure 4.1). The geographical coverage of the Convention was expanded to include internal waters, and the area of application was enlarged to the entire catchment area of the Baltic Sea.

The new Convention was augmented by setting up a Joint Comprehensive Environmental Action Programme (JCP) (see Auer and Nilenders 2001; Gutner 2002), which guided the activities of HELCOM countries during the 1990s and early 2000s until the BSAP was introduced as a guideline to activities in 2007.

In general, cooperation within HELCOM has proceeded rather smoothly, without many disputes or conflicts. Perhaps this is because of the strong scientific emphasis of the regime, which also can explain why the main challenges dealt with have been related to scientific aspects, like inconsistencies in monitoring, measurement and assessment.[14] Throughout the years, the basic obstacle to cooperation facing both Russian and Western analysts of water quality in Russian cities has been poor access to high-quality water monitoring data. Pollution amounts are commonly reported only at coarse geographic scales, a legacy of Soviet-era statistical practices (Trumbull 2007, p. 497). Illustrative of these problems is the story told by a Finnish expert: when they had the

Source: HELCOM 2004b. Reprinted with permission from the Finnish Environment
Institute SYKE and National Land Survey of Finland 2004.

*Figure 4.1   The Baltic Sea catchment area and sub-basins as defined for
              HELCOM Fourth Baltic Sea Pollution Load Compilation*

possibility to do their own nutrient monitoring in certain Russian points (for example, in the Neva estuary), they found that the figures reported by the Russian counterpart were sometimes far higher than those measured by the Finnish counterpart, sometimes far lower.[15] Another related controversial issue in cooperation has concerned the two different scientific approaches used for calculating permissible pollution load: in the West, loads at the end of the sewerage pipeline are measured, whereas the East has used the 'limitation of pollution in the recipient water body' approach (HELCOM 2004a, p. 10). This is related to Russian environmental regulations, which use the system of maximum allowable concentration as the basis of environmental norms. This may lead to a situation in which many enterprises dissolve wastewater in large amounts of water to ensure that concentration limits are not exceeded (see Kochtcheeva 2009, p. 169).

In the following two sections, we examine in greater detail activities within the HELCOM regime and the related Russian discussion during the 1990s and early years after the turn of the millennium on the one hand, and since about 2006 on the other.

1990s and Early 2000s: The Era of Practical Cooperation

In the Joint Comprehensive Environmental Action Programme (JCP) introduced in 1992, a list was prepared of 132 points and diffuse source 'hot spots' within the Baltic Sea catchment area that required environmental investments estimated at €10 billion. Most these hot spots concerned untreated or partially treated wastewater of municipalities and industries (VanDeveer 2011, p. 45); 95 of them were located in Eastern Europe and the former Soviet Union (Trumbull unpublished, p. 5). JCP implementation was conceived as a joint enterprise, with costs to be covered by both domestic and external sources, in the form of grants or long-term credits (Darst 2001, p. 74).

The progress achieved in implementation of the JCP during its first seven years (1993–99) was remarkable as regards municipal wastewater treatment, especially in the Baltic States and Poland (see HELCOM 1996). In Russia, the programme was less successful, with the exception of progress achieved in the city of St Petersburg, which had been the greatest single-point pollution source in the Baltic. There, joint efforts to develop the water sector of the city, a major hot spot on the HELCOM list, started in the early 1990s in bilateral cooperation between the government of Finland and the water and sewage utility, St Petersburg Vodokanal. During the 1990s the governments of the UK, Sweden, and Denmark, and financial institutions such as the European Bank for Reconstruction and Development (EBRD) joined in activities under a large-scale investment programme aimed at improving environmental conditions and the quality of water supply and sewage disposal. The construction of the south west wastewater treatment plant, a project originally launched in the mid-1980s, was restarted as part of this programme in 2000. In addition to Vodokanal's own share, the construction project was financed through subordinated loans from various international financial organizations and grant financing from the governments of Finland and Sweden. Other projects conducted under the programme include the construction of a sludge incineration plant, the introduction of chemical-biological phosphorus removal and the construction of major collector sewers.

The involvement of international partners in the development of the St Petersburg water sector has continued in the form of the Neva programme, a large-scale project of total €560 million, under the Northern Dimension Environmental Partnership (NDEP) portfolio, funded by various organizations.[16] As declared by Russian Prime Minister Dmitry Medvedev at the international Baltic Summit in St Petersburg in April 2013, the programme was nearing completion, as some 98 per cent of the wastewater of the city is currently being purified, and levels of nutrients in the purified water are in compliance with HELCOM recommendations.[17]

In Kaliningrad, however, water sector cooperation has been far less successful. Even as of spring 2014, the wastewaters of the city residents (400 000) are discharged without any treatment. An international agreement on constructing municipal wastewater treatment facilities was reached in 1999 (Darst 2001, p. 84) but by 2013, the construction work (originally started in 1976!) was still not complete. After many delays and changes, the construction work continued in international cooperation in 2009 as a NDEP project funded by the governments of Russia, Sweden and Denmark as well as the EBRD, the Nordic Investment Bank (NIB) and the Nordic Environment Finance Corporation (NEFCO).[18] The latest news is that because of disagreement between partners, the project was halted again in 2014.[19] To sum up, about 15 out of 34 HELCOM hot spots in Russia were eliminated between 1992 and 2011, and most were related to the St Petersburg water sector. Other projects basically failed. Nechiporuk et al. (2011, p. 52) explain the reasons as follows: lack of coordination among the various levels of administration involved in Baltic Sea protection in Russia; the absence of an effective environmental monitoring system at the federal and regional levels; insufficient knowledge or technology; and a weak civil society unable to put pressure on politicians and the authorities. In the St Petersburg water sector, these problems could be avoided, one crucial factor being the early engagement between Western and local actors.

Storyline I: cooperation is an opportunity to modernize

The main storyline characterizing Russia's HELCOM participation during the 1990s and early years of the new millennium saw cooperation first and foremost as an opportunity for municipal industries to establish their own contacts across the border and to launch cooperation projects with foreign partners. A quote from Felix Karmazinov, Director-General of the St Petersburg water and sewage utility Vodokanal, is illustrative of this point:

> What helped us see the light at the end of the tunnel in the 1990s was co-operation with our closest neighbour, Finland. We are grateful to the Finns for their moral support. They also helped us discover modern water treatment technologies and how to raise loans with international financial institutions.[20]

According to this storyline, cooperation with the Baltic Sea environment brings economic benefits to Russian actors in the form of grants and investments, as well as in the form of the transfer of know-how and institutional capacities. As noted by a representative of St Petersburg Vodokanal, its engagement with foreign partners has also 'increased the autonomy of the utility so that it nowadays is self-sufficient both in administrative and financial terms', and the utility now works as a consultant for authorities in matters related to environmental management, cost recovery and public relations.[21]

In this storyline, cooperation is presented as a *win-win* situation; the Russian opinion is that also Western companies benefit economically from modernization projects in Russia. One of the biggest achievements of the cooperation – the construction of the South West wastewater treatment plant in St Petersburg – was the first project in Russia to be conducted using the public-private partnership (PPP) model, which benefits all sides of cooperation, also economically. Since then, the PPP has been emphasized by many Russians. For example, the 2013 Baltic Sea Summit in St Petersburg (see below) was devoted to the advancement of the PPP approach, strongly underlined by the closing speech of Prime Minister Medvedev:

> The final goal of us is to form a common Baltic space on the basis of a partnership between the states and private actors, a space of cooperation for mutual benefits, which is necessary for health and well-being of all people living on the shores of the Baltic Sea.[22]

The summit resulted in the St Petersburg Initiative, which emphasizes the importance of PPPs in cooperation.[23] In sum, the storyline emphasizes that throughout the history of such cooperation, all counterparts have benefited also in economic terms.[24]

Storyline II: 'silly' Western concerns . . .
The second storyline, partly but not entirely overlapping with the first one, also supports cooperation, seeing it mainly as a way to obtain funding from the partners. This storyline differs from the first one as the issues addressed by HELCOM are not seen as so worrisome. Indeed, Western concerns are to some extent regarded as 'silly'.[25] Eutrophication, for example, is not considered a serious problem, because 'nobody has ever died of it'.[26] As noted by Felix Karmazinov: 'When the main now working treatment facilities were designed, no one in our country thought much about the need to remove nitrogen and phosphorus from wastewater'.[27] Removal of these nutrients, however, was a main concern for the regime and the Western partners who helped in the wastewater projects. For the Russian counterpart, the main motivation was to modernize the water sector in general, with improved water supply and overall purification of sewage from various contaminants. There were other, more local problems related to the environment and wastes that were of concern during the 1990s and early 2000s – like the construction of the anti-flooding dam and new landfills in the city of St Petersburg (see below), and the problem of waste management in the Kaliningrad region.

According to this storyline, the Baltic Sea may be in bad condition, but the Western concerns are futile because there is not much that can be done to improve the situation.

> I have nothing negative to say against the restrictions. Perhaps . . . Well, there is nothing wrong, nothing bad in them. Eh . . . But to what extent that helps, cannot say. Because there are also other sources of pollution, and so . . .[28]

Even if this storyline does not see the cooperation as helping the environment very much, it is advocated that Western concerns should be taken advantage of in the form of environmental subsidization and investments. This storyline, dominant during the 1990s and early 2000s, is still in active use, and is criticized by Russian NGOs in particular. For example, one NGO representative held that the Federal Target Programme for the Development of the Kaliningrad Region until 2015, which promises the introduction of wastewater treatment facilities by 2015, is 'mainly aimed at boosting the investment appeal of the regions, rather than responding to the concerns of the residents'.[29] Another example from Kaliningrad is provided by the programme for environmental improvement of the territory of the Kaliningrad region 2008–12, according to which all measures under the programme 'should be introduced in the framework of cross-border cooperation' – that is, funded at least partly from abroad (Nechiporuk and Nozhenko 2010, p. 113).

From 2004 Onwards

The accession of Finland and Sweden, the Baltic republics and Poland to the EU in 1995 and 2004 made all Baltic coastal countries, except Russia, members of the EU. The supranational character of the EU has implications for the environmental governance of the Baltic Sea, affecting also the activities of the HELCOM regime. In this context, HELCOM sees itself as 'a catalyst for regional and supranational policymaking' and as a 'spokesperson' for the Baltic Sea in the EU (Brusendorff 2006, p. 66). Main tasks of the regime are seen as the provision of information about the health of the marine ecosystem, and about the efficiency of measures taken to protect the sea.

The BSAP, a tailor-made regional application of the ecosystem approach to the management of the Baltic Sea environment, was adopted at the HELCOM Ministerial Meeting in Krakow, Poland, in 2007 (HELCOM 2007). All coastal countries are committed to the implementation of the plan through national implementation programmes (NIPs), introduced at the 2010 Ministerial meeting in Moscow (HELCOM 2013a). There are four segments in the BSAP: eutrophication, hazardous substances, biodiversity and maritime activities. The ultimate aim of the plan is to achieve a Baltic Sea with good environmental status by 2021. The main emphasis is on the goal of a 'Baltic Sea unaffected by eutrophication'. This goal is defined by five specific ecological objectives, including a natural level of algal blooms and natural oxygen levels. In order to achieve clear water, inputs of phosphorous and nitrogen to the Baltic Sea must be cut by about 42 per cent and 18 per cent, respectively (HELCOM 2007). The BSAP also proposes provisional 'country-wise' annual nutrient input reduction targets for nitrogen and phosphorus so that the main bulk of reductions will concern the Baltic Sea proper; the Gulf of Bothnia was considered to have good ecological status and thus not in need of reductions.[30]

As nutrient input reductions so far have been achieved mainly through improvements at major point sources, like sewage treatment plants and industrial wastewater outlets, the BSAP places special emphasis on diffuse sources of nutrients, like runoff from over-fertilized agricultural lands. Implementation of the EU Water Framework Directive is seen as among the most significant regulative measures for realization of the plan; however, that instrument excludes Russia, as a non-EU member state. The main funding sources for the actions described in the BSAP are national budgets and EU structural and cohesion funds. In addition, the Northern Dimension Environmental Partnership (NDEP) Fund and international financial organizations provide funding for individual projects aimed at BSAP implementation, especially in Russia.[31]

As part of the BSAP commitment, Russia introduced its National Programme for the Rehabilitation and Recovery of the Baltic Sea Ecosystem in 2010, as well as a specially targeted federal programme to provide appropriate federal funding for implementation.[32] These programmes aim at improving wastewater treatment so that 100 per cent of wastewater will be treated in 2020; also measures targeted at decreasing agricultural runoff are set in the programmes. The main goals are the reconstruction of wastewater treatment facilities, Krasny Bor landfill, building a port depot in Kaliningrad and disposal of untreated agricultural wastewater in the Leningrad region. Total funding allocated for the programme is 145 billion roubles.[33] According to Leonid Korovin, representing HELCOM in Russia, the best indicator of Russia's priorities with regard to implementation of the BSAP is the amount of money that Russia is to spend in accordance with its national programme. In this priority list, reducing nutrient load by constructing and reconstructing wastewater treatment plants gets first priority, followed by the reduction of wastewater from ships.[34]

Russia has expressed its satisfaction with the BSAP. In particular, the technical-scientific nature of the plan (rather than direct political pressure) is greatly appreciated.[35] Russia accepted the BSAP without any major demands (although it managed to achieve certain changes in the final text with regard to banning the use of phosphates in detergents and mercury).[36] In general, Russia's activeness in HELCOM has been constantly growing; notably, Russia hosted the HELCOM presidency in 2008–10. However, Russia has resisted some developments, such as the declaration of the Baltic Sea as a Particularly Sensitive Sea Area (PSSA) by the International Maritime Organization (IMO). PSSA status is accorded to sea areas deemed to be especially vulnerable to risks caused by transport and other harm. In these areas, specific measures are used to control maritime activities, for example, routing measures and stricter requirements of discharge and equipment for ships such as oil tankers. Since 2004, PSSA status has applied to all parts of the Baltic Sea with the exception of Russian waters; as Russia opposed such status, its territorial waters were exempted from the area (see Gritsenko 2013).

In addition, Russia has consistently opposed the declaration of the NOx Emission Control Area (NECA) status of the Baltic Sea as of 2016 in HELCOM. This led to the issue being dropped from the HELCOM Ministerial Declaration in October 2013, despite earlier plans to submit the application on the Baltic Sea NECA to the IMO soon.[37] Russian arguments for not applying for the status relate to technological issues: in the view of Russian experts, there exist no efficient technologies for shipping under NECA requirements.[38] These requirements would basically imply tighter NOx emission standards for vessel traffic in the Baltic Sea.

This Russian resistance can be understood, since the volume of Russian transport in the Baltic Sea has exploded since the mid-1990s. Energy transport originating from Russia increased eight-fold, from 20 million tonnes to 160 million tonnes, between 1995 and 2009 (Brunila and Storgård 2012). The figure is expected to continue to rise, exceeding 250 million tonnes by 2015. Almost one-fourth of all oil production of Russia is transported through the Gulf of Finland in the Baltic Sea. Russia has concentrated its energy transport to the Baltic Sea, seeing the region as safer than southern routes and thus guaranteeing Russian oil and gas access to the European market (see Hänninen and Rytkönen 2004). Most important in the chain of Russian energy transport in the Baltic Sea is Primorsk, the biggest oil port of the Baltic Sea and the endpoint of the Baltic Pipeline System (BPS) in the eastern edge of the Gulf of Finland (Helle and Kuikka 2010, p. 191). Nord Stream, an offshore natural gas pipeline from Vyborg in Russia to Greifswald in Germany, inaugurated in 2011, forms an important part of Russian energy export in the Baltic. As energy transportation is a vital issue for the Russian economy, it is hardly surprising that Russia was particularly active in developing the maritime activities segment of the HELCOM BSAP and has devoted special attention to the environmental aspects of energy projects.

Storyline I: victory of science
According to this storyline, cooperation on the Baltic Sea protection is a victory of science: the solid scientific basis on which cooperation is built on makes it participation worthwhile. The BSAP in particular is praised for being 'based on solid and reliable scientific knowledge'. 'The Baltic Sea Action Plan is very carefully prepared and can be regarded as the victory of science (. . .) It is not just another political declaration, like the one at the 1980s: everybody has to decrease 50 per cent'.[39] And this storyline explains why HELCOM cooperation is so highly appreciated in Russia. As this cooperation is based on scientific facts, there can surely be nothing political about it.

This storyline defines environmental cooperation for the Baltic Sea as primarily a scientific task. The idea is reflected in the view that '(t)he problem (of eutrophication of the Baltic Sea) should, of course, be solved by specialists (and not by the general public), because it has very little to do with the ordinary citizen'.[40] The preservation of biodiversity through developing a network of specially protected nature areas, including the establishment of the Ingermanland Nature Reserve in 2010, is part of Russia's contribution to the Baltic Sea cooperation, seen as first and foremost a scientific project.

The storyline is facilitated also by the idea that, most importantly, the Baltic Sea environment would benefit from educating the people.

Interviewees and media alike give a simple and similar answer to the question of what should be done in Russia to help the Baltic Sea environment: *educate, educate, educate.* Indeed, the main focus of activity of most Russian environmental NGOs is on educational activities and raising environmental awareness about the Baltic Sea among schoolchildren.[41] There is an evident link between the view that Baltic Sea environmental cooperation is based on solid scientific knowledge and the need to educate people on the basis of this knowledge.

Storyline II: cooperation makes Russia a 'laggard'

Some actors hold that, in Baltic Sea environmental cooperation, Western countries have always decided what should be done and how, treating their Russian counterpart as a 'fall guy' and laggard in environmental protection. Take the words of one scientist:

> Western partners . . . tend to dramatize the role of Russia for the degradation of the Baltic Sea. And downplay their own role. It often happens that they put heavy requirements on Russia and lessen their own burden. This applies to Finns, Polish, and other countries in HELCOM.[42]

The storyline goes on to prove that Russia is no worse than the rest of the countries:

> For some reason they think that abroad everything is much safer, abroad these activities, such as oil refining near the ports and water, are ok, but in Russia – no, no. Why? I ask. Because we are so Russian, we always have that 'human factor' playing a role, and something always goes wrong. But I think that also in Russia we have brilliant people, specialists, and all those contracts, requirements that apply to Europe – all this can be realized in Russia, too.[43]

As part of the storyline there are also, naturally and rightly so, boasts about the development of the St Petersburg wastewater treatment: here Russia meets 'the HELCOM standards for wastewater'[44] and is no more an indicator of laggardness. This storyline also includes the view that the USSR was actually the first country in the world to set limits on discharges of various types of industrial effluents (see Kochtcheeva 2009, p. 172). Water quality standards – maximum allowable concentrations (MACs) for water pollution – have existed well before the HELCOM regime, ever since the 1940s. More to the point, although without specifying any exact measures, 'the Russian Law on Protection of Nature (1960) required all organizations that had an effect on water bodies to build purification facilities, and prohibited putting new enterprises into operation that would not ensure sewage treatment' (ibid., p. 153).

This storyline also tries to bring out the deficiencies of other countries in their Baltic Sea policies, especially with regard to their ability to fulfil the requirements of the BSAP.[45] For example, the Russian Ministry of Natural Resources issued a press release when a Polish fertilizer plant was identified as a major source of nutrient pollution into the Baltic Sea:

> The Russian Ministry is concerned about the information on the leakage of phosphorus into the water basin of the Baltic Sea near the city of Gdansk in Poland . . . We expect that the Polish side will, as a part of the obligations of the Helsinki Convention, immediately take all necessary actions to stop the leakage and minimize the negative impacts on the Baltic Sea.[46]

This did not happen when a similar point-source was found in a fertilizer plant in Kingisepp, in northwest Russia, in winter 2012. Quite the contrary: when a Finnish expert working for the HELCOM project 'Balthazar' revealed a major point-source of nutrients there, Russian actors declared that there was nothing wrong with the plant. Leonid Korovin, head of HELCOM in Russia, stated: 'The claim that the Fosforit plant is polluting the Baltic Sea is rash and incorrect. Today it is obvious that the source of phosphorus in the Luga River is not located on the territory of the plant'.[47] The Russian Ministry of Natural Resources, in turn, commented on the case merely by requesting the Finnish counterpart to 'carefully investigate the activities of the Finnish expert in the case'.[48]

Thus we see that this storyline is supported by efforts to downplay and hide problems in Russia. The storyline also emphasizes the positive and cooperative behaviour of Russian actors: in the abovementioned case, EuroChem, the owner of the Fosforit plant, was highly praised in the Russian media: for instance, '(t)he company EuroChem once again demonstrates openness and transparency in its activity: it invited all leading media from Finland and wanted to promote an open dialogue'.[49]

Storyline III: Russia IS a laggard
This storyline, in contrast to the previous one, centres on blaming Russia for being a laggard and not behaving in a civilized way in Baltic Sea cooperation. Some actors are ashamed of, for example, what happened in the Kaliningrad water sector prior to 2009, about Russia's 'drain' of a Swedish grant of €37 million in the process.[50] They are ashamed of poor wastewater treatment and other environmental problems that have not been dealt with.

> I cannot understand, I simply cannot get it. [Poor wastewater treatment] is a very clear problem, visible to all. At the same time, our governor finds the money for building roads – gigantic roads by the way – finds the money from the city budget . . .[51]

The storyline underlines that HELCOM does good work and its provisions are implemented in Russian legislation – but domestic implementation is the problem.

> We have these norms, for example, concerning the allowable concentration of nutrients in the purified wastewater. But what do we do with the norms, when municipal wastewater is not purified at all?[52]

The domestic authorities are accused of not caring about the environment, or, if the authorities at the local level do care, then it is the federal authorities who ignore local problems. Environmental NGOs criticize the priorities of the authorities, for caring not about environmental aspects, but investments and money:

> The government of the Leningrad region ... is interested in big investors, mainly. So the projects need to be 'sold' to them by talking the language of money, not the language of ecology.[53]

Contributing to this storyline, some Russian actors criticize foreign partners for having very loose policies as regards cooperation with Russia, enabling the Russian counterpart to behave as a laggard by misusing the resources. As one interviewee noted:

> [i]t is always like that with (HELCOM) projects. It is possible to successfully finish the project and then fully forget about it without putting anything into practice. Why? Why is that so? Projects and programmes have themselves been very good, but ... still.[54]

Therefore, the storyline encompasses the idea that funding comes from all parties, and also from the Russian side.

> I don't agree with the argument that foreigners should pay more because they have more money. No! I think that we should be equal here. I think that this needs to be solved in the following way: it is the one who has polluted the most who pays the most.[55]

Storyline IV: cooperation helps Russia to balance EU dominance in the Baltic Sea region

The storyline, according to which cooperation helps Russia to balance EU dominance in the Baltic Sea region, emerged after the Baltic States and Poland joined the EU in 2004, so that eight of the nine Baltic Sea coastal countries now belong to the Union. Perhaps the most striking example of this storyline is offered by a press release of Minpriroda, issued after the opening ceremony of Russia's HELCOM presidency. In that release, it was suggested by Igor Maidanov, head of international relations department at the Russian Ministry of Natural Resources, that the CIS[56] would be accepted as a HELCOM contracting party, since the European Commission also is a member.[57] Drawing on this storyline, some interpreted the participation of Prime Minister Putin in the Baltic Sea Action Summit in Helsinki in 2010 as a sign intended to demonstrate the power of Russia in defining the future of the region.[58]

In other words, this storyline emphasizes the roles of HELCOM and the Council of the Baltic Sea States (CBSS) in balancing the dominance of the EU in the Baltic Sea region.[59] Russian actors praise these regional institutions for helping to stabilize the region and to create conditions for its dynamic development. The significance of HELCOM for Russia was demonstrated when Russia organized a Baltic Sea Summit for state leaders in St Petersburg in 2013. This event was commented on by Vadim Sivkov, director of the Atlantic Department of the Institute of Oceanology, who underscored that after the summit, '(t)he Europeans no more think that the Baltic Sea is the internal sea of the European Union'.[60] Also the strong commitment of Russia to the implementation of the Baltic Sea Action Plan can be linked to this storyline. As commented by Leonid Korovin, Russian representative in HELCOM from the organization Ekologia i Biznes:

> ... there are no political or economic sanctions for not fulfilling the programme. But prestige, authority and the possibility for cooperation with our European colleagues suffers if the requirements are not fulfilled.[61]

Storyline V: environmental cooperation as a tool for promoting energy export, economic cooperation and general confidence in the region

Storyline V, which defines environmental cooperation as a tool for promoting energy export, economic cooperation and general confidence in the Baltic Sea region, is strongly supported by the main documents guiding marine policy in Russia: the *Development Strategy of Maritime Activities of the Russian Federation to 2030* (2010),[62] and the *Maritime Doctrine of the Russian Federation 2020*.[63] Both documents mention the protection of marine environments in the territorial waters of Russia among the strategic goals but focus explicitly on the development of maritime transportation. The Maritime Doctrine defines the long-term objectives of Russia's marine policy in the Baltic Sea as follows:

- 'development of coastal port infrastructure, the upgrade of maritime trade and mixed (river–sea) navigation;
- creating the conditions for sustained economic cooperation with countries in the Baltic region, joint management of marine natural resources, with comprehensive confidence-building measures in all fields of maritime activity;
- settlement of issues related to the delimitation of maritime areas and continental shelf between the Russian Federation, opposite and adjacent states;
- economic and military security of the Kaliningrad region of the Russian Federation, the development of maritime transportation;
- creation of conditions, including those with the capacity of the region for the home and use of marine capabilities, ensuring the protection of sovereignty, sovereign and international rights of the Russian Federation in the Baltic Sea'.[64]

These objectives show that environmental cooperation and joint resource management are seen as being among the main instruments for sustained economic and energy cooperation and confidence-building in the Baltic Sea region.

The storyline is augmented by NGO criticisms of Russia's behaviour in HELCOM. Especially during the Russian HELCOM presidency, many of the country's NGOs were dissatisfied with Russia's actions; they felt that the Russian leadership saw the Baltic Sea only as a 'fast-developing transport corridor' and that the Russian HELCOM presidency focused solely on this aspect.[65] For example, according to the journal *Ekologia i Zizn*, the Russian HELCOM presidency was all about lobbying the Nord Stream gas pipeline, nothing else.[66] In addition, came accusations that the most extensive parts of Russia's National Implementation Programme of the BSAP were related to the use of port infrastructure.[67]

Indicative of this storyline is the view that the Nord Stream project has been used to demonstrate Russia's commitment to environmental cooperation and of its ability to follow international procedures and standards.[68] For example, Prime Minister Putin emphasized at the Baltic Sea Action Summit in 2010 how high environmental standards were applied in the construction of the Nord Stream gas pipeline.[69] Also in other instances the Russian leadership has stressed its adherence to the highest environmental standards, as with regard to oil fields near Kaliningrad.[70] In general, this storyline features great emphasis on the environmental safety of Russia's new energy infrastructure. This includes promoting Primorsk, Russia's single most important outlet, which started operations in 2007, as 'the ecologically safest Russian port'.[71]

EMERGING DISCOURSES

The above delineated storylines encapsulate the core of Russian discourses on cooperation. The discourses we have identified here can be called *benefit discourse, great power discourse, partnership discourse, and environmental discourse*. These discourses are overlapping in the sense that the storylines are used in many of the discourses, and one discourse can also bring together several storylines.

Benefits Discourse

One recurrent theme in Russian ways of perceiving and talking about cooperation on the protection of the Baltic Sea concerns the various *benefits*. According to this benefit discourse, cooperation should be something that brings benefits to Russia. Although less straightforward than in the case of climate policy, Baltic Sea cooperation has been valued for the political and financial benefits that it brings. According to Robert Darst (2001), early Soviet participation in the Helsinki Convention was motivated primarily by political interests. At the time of the initial negotiations on the Convention, the Soviet leadership was pressing for Western recognition of the German Democratic Republic (see also Räsänen and Laakkonen 2008),[72] and was also reluctant to take serious obligations under the Convention. Because of this reluctance on the part of Russia, coastal waters were excluded from the Convention – which made it totally meaningless with regard to land-based pollution.

In the 1990s, the benefit discourse shifted to an emphasis on the financial benefits of cooperation, including investments by foreign partners into Russian environmental projects. The St Petersburg water and sewage utility Vodokanal is the best-known example here: ever since the early 1990s it has benefited from cooperation in the form of direct subsidies, technical support and international loans worth several hundred million euros (see Vesitalous 2012). Indirectly, the utility has benefited from cooperation also in terms of power; cooperation has also served as a way of gaining independence from the domestic authorities. And of course the residents of St Petersburg have benefited from cooperation in terms of improved water supply and wastewater management.

The benefit discourse has been supported also by the West, where the cooperation has been seen as a profitable deal. As Darst (2001, p. 72) notes:

[Western] companies stood to benefit from the sale of the necessary purification technology to aid recipients, and from government economic officials who viewed state-subsidized exports of environmental technology as a way to boost their recession-wracked national economies (Finland in particular).

It has also been less expensive for Western HELCOM countries to help the Eastern countries to curb their emissions than to take domestic measures, because they had already undertaken the easiest and cheapest environmental investments at home in the 1970s and 1980s.

With regard to financial benefits, cooperation is in some cases (as with St Petersburg Vodokanal) seen as a win-win situation, and in others as beneficial only to Russia. In the latter view, the basic idea is that Russia is a sly actor that takes advantage of 'silly Western concerns' in the form of economic benefits – the Baltic Sea environment itself is by no means a matter of major concern. One explanation here may be that environmental problems and risks are usually defined as health issues in Russia – and as long as there is no direct link to human health, the problem is not considered serious (see, for example, Kochtcheeva 2009, p. 153). Hydrography supports this view: due to the water circulation patterns in the Baltic Sea, nutrients originating in Russia and Poland end up mainly on the Finnish and Swedish coasts, accelerating the growth of algae there. Thus, Russian shores are not as polluted as some others, and the problem is less visible there (see Pihlajamäki and Tynkkynen 2011c).

Significant economic benefits can be gained for Russian energy exports. In general, cooperation on the Baltic Sea environment is held to facilitate energy exports by improving the environmental image of Russia's energy transport as well as through increased general confidence. This is linked to using environmental cooperation to bring image benefits through environmental actions in the field of energy infrastructure. Non-commitment would threaten the benefits in terms of prestige, authority and further possibilities for cooperation. Also Russia's HELCOM presidency was justified within the benefits discourse; it was beneficial for Russia to hold the presidency, as that made it possible to promote the Nord Stream gas pipeline and its environmental image. Even the shame that some actors feel about, for instance, untreated urban wastewater can be interpreted within benefits discourse: 'a civilized country treats its wastewaters' – and so, if cooperation helps Russia to construct treatment plants, that brings image benefits of Russia as a 'civilized' country.

The benefit discourse is opposed to the strongest of the discourses inside Russia: as shown in the storylines explicated above, Russian NGOs especially criticize their compatriots for seeking financial benefits from the cooperation and using environmental forums for other purposes, like promoting Russian energy exports.

Great Power Discourse

A recurrent theme throughout the history of the Baltic Sea environmental protection regime has been Russia's role as a great power and the attendant geopolitical interests. Although the term 'great power' is seldom used in the context of the Baltic Sea cooperation, the presence of the idea is evident and frames Russia's behaviour in the cooperation. Geopolitical interests were particularly noteworthy in the beginning of the cooperation in the 1970s, and then re-emerged after the enlargement of the EU in 2004. This has been reflected in greater emphasis on the importance of HELCOM and the CBSS *vis-à-vis* the growing influence of the EU on environmental policies in the Baltic Sea region, and Russia has stepped up its activity in these institutions.

This recent activeness is partly related to new attitudes towards international cooperation in general: since Vladimir Putin's first presidential term from 2000 onwards, Russia has actively sought to revive its great power status through 'soft power' (see Chapter 2). This resulted in a strengthening of Russia's role in various international organizations, including HELCOM. The geopolitical motivations for participation are openly articulated, and cooperation is seen as game in which the balance of power is the main logic of operation. This explains also why the Russian leadership has recently activated and started to participate in a range of activities organized within the framework of the Baltic Sea environmental cooperation. The holding of the Baltic Sea Summit in St Petersburg in 2013 can be understood as part of the great power discourse: to demonstrate the power of Russia in the Baltic Sea region and to combat the EU dominance, as was openly stated in several speeches given at the meeting.

The great power discourse underlines Russia's greatness: for example, how Russia has always fulfilled its obligations within the Helsinki Convention and followed all the recommendations given within HELCOM. More generally, Russians like to emphasize their natural resources and ecological 'reserves'; in the Baltic case, this includes a focus on nature protection, nature reserves and the biodiversity Russia is 'offering' to the rest of the region. The great power discourse also explains why environmental flaws, like the nutrient leakage from the *Fosforit* fertilizer plant in Kingisepp, are ignored or even denied, so as not to tarnish the great power image. Also the occasions in which environmental NGOs collaborating with Western actors (for example, Ecodefense in Kaliningrad) have been accused of espionage become more understandable when seen from this viewpoint. Russia needs to protect its great power status, national interests and sovereignty; therefore, Russia cannot allow its image and prestige to be harmed through negative publicity or intimating that it cannot manage its own affairs. That Russia should be seen as an environmental laggard is a violation of the great power image, and by no means acceptable. But if things go so far that this happens – that Russia is accused of being a laggard – then Russia, as a great power, simply ignores it.

The discourse can explain many matters that at first glance seem odd. For example, Russia did not join the Particularly Sensitive Sea Areas (PSSA) regime, although it has been seeking to ensure the quality of oil transport, which seems extremely important for Russia's image today. Daria Gritsenko explains this within the broader context of political confrontation and great power discourse towards the EU: in this context, the strategy of the Russian government is not paradoxical (Gritsenko 2013). Similarly, Russia has been reluctant to comply with the restrictions on sulphur and nitrogen emissions of ships, which are vital issues for HELCOM[73] (see also Oldberg 2012, p. 37).

Partnership Discourse

According to the partnership discourse, cooperation should be something that unfolds between two (or more) equal partners. Similar to the great power discourse, then, the partnership discourse opposes the treatment of Russia as a laggard or recipient in cooperation. The partnership discourse underlines Russia's achievements in the environmental sector, and may include downplaying the achievements of others – but only in order to demonstrate that parties to cooperation are in fact equal. In that sense, the discourse differs from the great power discourse, which aims to demonstrate Russia's greatness and superiority. From a partnership point of view, one goal of cooperation can be the creation of partnerships; thus, the results of cooperation are measured not only by figures but also by assessing the cooperation process itself. Also strongly evident in this discourse is the idea that environmental cooperation is one way to build general confidence in the region.

The discourse dislikes Western *Besserwissers* [know-it-alls] who come and tell Russia what should be done. Especially in the early years of the cooperation between St Petersburg Vodokanal and foreign partners, the former accused the latter of having a 'Besserwisser attitude': they came and told the Russians what to do, downplaying the knowledge of local actors (see Tynkkynen 2008b). To oppose this, staff at Vodokanal underlined the importance of a partnership attitude in the cooperation. Perhaps the easiest way to achieve partnership is to collaborate through practical projects: small and informal meetings, workshops, and working on a daily basis were in the Vodokanal case described as the best working methods of the partnership-based cooperation (ibid.). In such a partnership, people usually know each other personally – a point highly appreciated by Russians. The recent emphasis on public-private partnerships is indicative of the contemporary strength of the partnership discourse.

In sum, according to the partnership discourse, Russia is an equal partner in the cooperation, with equal decision-making rights. Such partnership empowers also the Russian side to define goals and strategies of cooperation, not merely comply with what is set by the other party. Moreover, it empowers Russia to contribute financially, and take care of its part of the costs. Partnership discourse is about having a pragmatic approach to cooperation: the idea is that cooperation on lower levels and on non-political issues facilitates confidence-building in general in the Baltic Sea region. Emphasizing the partnership approach is also beneficial from the perspective of Russian energy exports, as it underlines mutual independency and common needs in the Baltic Sea region.

Russia's marine policy shapes its actions regarding the Baltic Sea. Here we should note that the foreign policy concept of the Russian Federation, ratified by the President of Russia in February 2013, defines 'effective use of oceans' as one priority of Russia's international cooperation in the sphere of the economy and the environment.[74]

Environmental Discourse

At first glance, it may seem that there is no 'environmental' discourse evolving from the storylines. However, some elements of an environmental discourse can be found. As the storyline depicting Russia as a laggard indicates, some Russian actors really think that the environment is the main motivation in the cooperation (or at least should be) and that efforts should focus on remedying the environmental problems identified. Some supporters of the discourse hold that environmental cooperation on the Baltic Sea is needed primarily because the Russian environment is in poor shape, and Russia seems unable to take care of the environment by itself. And other supporters of the discourse see Russia as doing its job, striving for an environmentally healthier Baltic Sea alongside its cooperative partners.

However, the most serious problems of the Baltic Sea are defined in a different way from the partners, or the HELCOM regime, define them. This is evident in the storyline that Western concerns are 'silly' and are not shared by Russia. Also Roginko (1998, p. 588) notes that '. . . in Russia some environmental problems are regarded as "first class" problems because they attract the attention of the West. The significance of such problems within Russian policy is determined primarily by the response they cause abroad, and to a much lesser extent by their domestic impact'.

But this does not mean that the environment is not a domestic concern at all. In St Petersburg, for example, local issues not directly linked to the concerns of the international regime have received more attention than those raised by the regime and its experts. In the mid- and late-1980s as well as in the first half of the 1990s, the construction of a giant anti-flooding dam in Neva Bay near the city provoked massive public demonstrations and criticism (see, for example, Pryde 1995, p. 50; Trumbull 2007, p. 502). Later, a new landfill and port on the western shores of Vasilevskii Island and a new residential and commercial centre 'Baltic Pearl' along the previously undeveloped southern shoreline of Neva Bay and the Gulf of Finland evoked public criticism/concern (see Trumbull 2007, pp. 500–1).[75] In Kaliningrad, the waste problem has been the most heatedly discussed problem; it is often linked to the Baltic Sea environment by noting that shore areas in particular are basically like rubbish pits, '*svalki*'.[76]

Eutrophication, however, is seen as a serious problem only by a few. In the Russian press, untreated urban wastewater is often defined as the Baltic Sea environmental problem number one in Russia *as regards international cooperation*. What the wastewater does to the water (eutrophication, which the HELCOM regime defines as the most serious problem of the Baltic Sea) is rarely explained.[77] In other words, eutrophication as such is not seen as being of special concern: wastewater treatment is seen as primarily a management problem. Then again, there are those who share the environmental concern, but felt that there is not much that can be done by human effort. Supporters of that view belong to the minority, however.

The environment is a crucial theme in all discussions about the construction of the new energy infrastructure. Of course, underscoring the environmental safety of energy transport can be interpreted in the framework of all the other discourses, too, but also the environmental element is strongly present and cannot be ignored. The environmental aspects of energy infrastructure have been in focus not only in the international arena, but domestically as well. For example, the fairly hefty domestic debate on the environmental safety of the Nord Stream gas pipeline project included the Federal Duma in 2006–07, and the central and regional press.

The environmental discourse defines the main solutions to the problems as scientific-technical ones. It is widely held that the cooperation should take place on a scientific basis. The Russian proclivity for interpreting environmental problems as scientific problems can also explain why the HELCOM regime has throughout its history, and especially in the 1970s and early 1980s, been strongly favoured by Russian actors compared to certain other, more political regimes. Today, the Baltic Sea Action Plan is particularly appreciated in Russia because it is based on the principles of natural science. This idea supports the guiding principle of Russian environmental policy: the optimal use of nature according to rational scientific principles. This stems from Soviet-era environmental protection strategies but has effectively been carried into contemporary Russia as well (see Kochtcheeva 2009, p. 172). With regard to technological emphasis, energy infrastructure is an evident focus of environmental activities, as best available technology can readily be used in new construction. Similarly, wastewater treatment is in focus, as it too has fairly simple technological solutions. There is less discussion of other problems that require more fundamental changes and are in a more complex way interlinked with socio-economic issues. Indicative here is the Russian National Programme for BSAP implementation: the greatest amounts of funding are to be allocated to reducing nutrient loads, by constructing and reconstructing wastewater treatment plants.

CONCLUSIONS

When we examine discourses as compared with Russia's actual behaviour in the case of the Baltic Sea environmental cooperation, some discourses clearly stand out as stronger than others. First and foremost, Russia implements a pragmatic and practical approach to the cooperation. The Baltic Sea environment and international cooperation on its protection are not politicized in Russia, and Russia is relatively strongly committed to the HELCOM regime. It has implemented some HELCOM recommendations and other provisions, such as the BSAP, in its domestic policies. This reflects the benefits and partnerships discourses the most. Notwithstanding the strengthened role of Russia in the leadership and organization of HELCOM activities, the 'balance of power' rhetoric in which the dominance of the EU in the region is contested, is not so evident in Russia's behaviour. Instead, day-to-day collaboration and various bottom-up partnerships are favoured as the form of cooperation. In some cases, however, the great power stands up for its sovereignty and power of influence; the Kingisepp incident is one example.

When the Russian discourse on the Baltic Sea protection is compared with Western discourses, the discourses do not appear to differ from each other as much as in the case of climate policy, for example. Cooperation has not suffered from major political disputes; at least, political challenges have rarely attracted major publicity. As the analysis presented in this chapter has shown, there are certain differences in priority topics – the HELCOM regime emphasizes eutrophication, while Russia is more concerned about environmental threats associated with maritime transport – and in problem definitions. For example, the primary focus of current activities as defined by the HELCOM regime should be on the reduction of non-point nutrient pollution originating from agricultural activities, but Russia continues to emphasize wastewater treatment. However, that is a fully legitimate emphasis, as there are still many localities in Baltic Russia where wastewater treatment facilities are poorly developed. Russia can rather easily fulfil the BSAP requirements by improving its wastewater treatment.[78] The most recent cooperation projects in Russia, like those financed by the BSAP Fund,[79] are targeted at reducing the environmental load of agriculture. In sum, the differences in priorities have not affected the work of the regime very much.

The Baltic Sea case shows that environmental protection may at times be seen as a relatively easy field of interstate cooperation, and can therefore be used as a way of projecting an image of cooperativeness and eliciting cooperation in non-environmental areas of greater interest. A range of purely political factors encouraged governments to engage in cooperation for the Baltic Sea environment in the first place. The establishment of the HELCOM regime, an international institution for environmental protection, brought the Eastern and Western Blocs closer to each other, paving the way for stabilization of the political situation throughout northern Europe (Darst 2001; Räsänen and Laakkonen 2008). As Nathaniel Trumbull (unpublished, p. 10) has noted, by framing the tasks of the Convention as a scientific project in its initial years, HELCOM was able to move forward without significant political resistance from either side of the Iron Curtain. Although several scholars hold that Cold War competition gradually translated into genuine environmental cooperation in the Baltic Sea area (see, for example, Rytövuori 1980; Haas 1993), this chapter has shown that many elements of competition are still present today: the analysis of the Russian discourses reveals that much of Russia's strong commitment to the Baltic Sea protection can be explained by geopolitical and other foreign-policy factors – image, expression of goodwill or power of influence – rather than by environmental goals. This is in line with the idea of soft power, so important to the current Russian leadership.

Commitment to the environmental regime is facilitated by the importance of the Baltic Sea for Russia as an energy transport route. Here Russia cannot allow risks, as energy revenues are the main source of income for the country. Thus, tanker traffic quality is a strategic priority of the Russian state: anything that might threaten unimpeded energy transport – like a tanker accident or similar event – is against these strategic interests (see also Gritsenko 2013). Promoting an image of cooperativeness is beneficial for Russian energy sales in general. Russia has also pushed for economic cooperation and foreign investments in Russia as part of the Baltic Sea cooperation (see Oldberg 2012).

However, the approach emphasizing the 'image of cooperativeness' is by no means one-sided. Here we may note the statement by Göte Svenson, former chairman of HELCOM PITF[80] (HELCOM 2004a, p. 24):

> Any attempt to evaluate HELCOM activities – given the historic political realities of the Baltic Sea arena – must consider one specific feature of HELCOM cooperation: the complete lack of political tension between Contracting Parties when debating measures to attain the objectives of the Helsinki convention. This can in itself be seen as a success story, regardless of the resulting substantive achievements.

According to this view, the uninterrupted political dialogue between the member states can be seen as more valuable than the actual environmental impact of the HELCOM regime. Indeed, the uninterrupted dialogue has been regarded as more important than more stringent environmental policies or measures like a revision of the 1992 HELCOM hotspot list.[81] In short, the provisions of the regime have not been particularly heavy for Russia. Because of the non-political nature of the regime, it has focused mainly on scientific issues, which are easier to agree upon and can be considered politically neutral; also the ecosystem approach of the BSAP is very scientific in character. In sum, cooperation on the Baltic Sea environment has emerged as more of a diplomatic venue than a genuinely *environmental encounter*.

On a final note, Russia's participation in the Baltic Sea environmental protection regime may serve as a success story of its engagement in international environmental cooperation. That said, good relations without real targets and without any politics involved may not be sufficient in today's world. Now that the relations are well in place and the political and economic situation in the region fairly well established, it is time to move on to more practical cooperation with more stringent requirements, also within the Baltic Sea regime. As demonstrated by its environmental concern in the energy sector, Russia can take on serious environmental responsibilities, if there is pressure and motivation. Similar tools to put pressure and/or motivate can be employed in other sectors as well. And with that, we return to the partnership discourse: a crucial premise is that goals and strategies of cooperation are defined jointly, among equal partners.

NOTES

1. The empirical material is based on earlier research (for example, Tynkkynen 2008a, 2008b, 2011, 2013; Pihlajamäki and Tynkkynen 2011a, 2011b and 2011c) as well as

first-hand sources, including some 65 stakeholder interviews (with the management of the St Petersburg water utility Vodokanal in 2002–03; with NGO actors, researchers and local authorities in Russia 2003–04; with regional environmental authorities and researchers in Kaliningrad and St Petersburg in 2009; and with international partners and HELCOM experts in 2002–13). In addition, newspaper articles published in Russian regional and central press between 2006 and 2013 were analysed. The first part of the chapter explaining the formation of the regime draws predominantly on second-hand sources, like the illustrative analysis by Robert Darst (2001) on East-West cooperation on limiting the Baltic Sea pollution, and the historical overview by Tuomas Räsänen and Simo Laakkonen (2008).

2. Nefco (2013), 'The BSAP Fund. Speeding up the ecological restoration of the Baltic Sea', available at: www.nefco.org/sites/nefco.viestinta.org/files/The_BSAP_Fund.pdf (accessed 9 December 2013).

3. NDEP (2013), 'Kaliningrad water and environmental services rehabilitation', available at: http://ndep.org/projects/348/ (accessed 10 November 2013).

4. Postanovlenie ot 7 dekabria 2001 g. N. 866: 'O Federalnoi tselevoi programme razvitiia Kaliningradskoi Oblasti na period do 2015 goda', available at: http://docs.cntd.ru/document/901807531 (accessed 14 August 2014).

5. Altogether 1223 news items on the topic were published in the central and regional press (HELCOM/Baltic Sea) between 2006 and 2013. The peak came in 2010 (278), whereas 2006 had the lowest figure (54 items). As to region, Kaliningrad regional newspapers were more active in writing about the Baltic Sea than newspapers in the St Petersburg/Leningrad region. Most often, the news reported a related event, such as the Baltic Sea Action Summit in Helsinki in 2010, and the launch of the Kaliningrad regional development programme in 2008.

6. Interview with a representative of the Kaliningrad Regional Duma, Kaliningrad, 2009.

7. According to Kochtcheeva (2009), water use and protection are outlined only in a general manner in the 2006 Water Code, referring to various other laws and regulations, without identifying the agencies responsible for implementation. The code is said to include even direct impairments, including permitting the construction of wastewater facilities and storage near waterways (interview with NGO member, St Petersburg, 1998; see also Feldman and Blokov 2012, p. 28.

8. Interview with a representative of the Kaliningrad regional environmental authorities, Kaliningrad, 2009.

9. Interview with a Finnish expert on cooperation, Helsinki, 2013.

10. Interview with an NGO member, Kaliningrad, 2009.

11. Interview with two NGO members, Kaliningrad 2009, St Petersburg, 2011.

12. The Convention entered into force in 1980, following ratification by all member countries.

13. After ratification, the new convention entered into force on 17 January 2000; Russia ratified in 1998. Ratification was not preceded by any remarkable political debate in Russia.

14. Interview with HELCOM expert, Helsinki, 2011.

15. Interview with a Finnish expert, Helsinki, 2009.

16. NIB (2012), 'Good progress of the St. Petersburg Neva programme', available at: www.nib.int/news_publications/cases_and_feature_stories/1132/good_progress_of_the_st_petersburg_neva_programme (accessed 18 September 2012).

17. *Itar-Tass*, 5 April 2013: 'Strany Baltii dolzhny stremitsia k formirovaniu edinogo prostranstva gosudarstvenno-chastnogo partnerstva – Medvedev'.

18. NDEP (2013), 'Kaliningrad water and environmental services rehabilitation', available at: http://ndep.org/projects/348/ (accessed 10 November 2013).

19. Heli Saavalainen (2013), 'Kaliningradin puhdistamo käyttöön vasta 2014', *Helsingin Sanomat*, 20 April 2013.

20. Director General of Vodokanal Felix Karmazinov, in NIB Bulletin, June 2008.

21. Interview with a deputy director of Vodokanal SpB, St Petersburg 2002; see also Vodokanal (2001).

22. Press conference of Dmitry Medvedev on the Baltic Sea (in Russian), available at: http://archive.government.ru/stens/23750/index.html (accessed 5 December 2013).
23. For eample, *Itar-Tass*, 10 April 2013: 'Forum Baltiiskogo moria'.
24. Such as representative of the Russian marine register Olga Sazonova, according to *Izvestiya*, 25 March 2013.
25. Interview with an NGO member, Kaliningrad, 2009.
26. This is a common reaction when Russian colleagues are asked about their perceptions of eutrophication.
27. See Karmazinov 2010.
28. Interview with a NGO member, St Petersburg, 2011.
29. Interview with a NGO member, Kaliningrad, 2009.
30. The targets were corrected at the HELCOM Ministerial Conference in Copenhagen in October 2013: see HELCOM 2013b.
31. NDEP (2013), 'Successful partnership delivering concrete results for the Northern Dimension Policy: 2013', update available at. http://ndep.org/wp-content/uploads/NDEP-brochure-2013.pdf (accessed 10 November 2013).
32. Ekologia i Biznes (2010), '*Rossiiskaia natsionalnaia programma mer po ozdorovleniiu i reabilitatsii ekosistemy Baltiiskogo moria*', St Petersburg, Ekologia i Biznes.
33. For example, *Zelenyi Mir*, 12 November 2010: 'Do 2020 goda Rossiia'.
34. Personal communication with HELCOM expert, December 2013.
35. Interview with scientist, St Petersburg, 2009.
36. Personal communication with a HELCOM expert, December 2013.
37. See: www.eft.com/freight-transport/helcom-ministerial-declaration-omits-neca-status-baltic-sea-2016 (accessed 31 October 2013).
38. Konstantin Palnikov, Director of Russian Federation Transport Ministry's Department of State Policy for Marine and River Transport, eft.com, 17 October 2013, see: www.eft.com/freight-transport/helcom-ministerial-declaration-omits-neca-status-baltic-sea-2016 (accessed 31 October 2013).
39. Interview with a scientist, Kaliningrad, 2009.
40. Interview with an environmental authority, Kaliningrad, 2009.
41. Interviews with NGO representatives in Kaliningrad and St Petersburg 2009; see also Tynkkynen 2006.
42. Interview with a scientist, St Petersburg, 2009.
43. Interview with an NGO member, Kaliningrad, 2009.
44. For example, *IA Regnum* 12 December 2012: 'Za 5 let peterburgskii vodokanal likvidiroval 90 priamyh vypuskov ctochnyh vod'.
45. For example, *Itar-tass*, 23 March 2010: 'Nekotorye strany Baltiki comnevaiutsia v dostizhimosti kriteriev HELCOM, no RF svoi obiazatelstva vypolnit'.
46. *RIA Novosti*, 26 July 2013: 'Minprirody Rossii opasaetsia zagriazneniia Baltiiskogo moria popavshim v reki Pol'shi fosforom'.
47. *Vremia Kingisepp*, 1 February 2012: 'Mnogo shuma iz nichego, ili proby vody byli sdelany v prisutstvii strogih gostei'.
48. Representative of the Ministry of Foreign Affairs Aleksandr Lukashevich according to *Itar-Tass*, 23 April 2012.
49. *Vremia Kingisepp*, 20 June 2012: 'Spasem planetu obshchimi usiliiami!'.
50. For example, interview with an NGO member, Kaliningrad, 2009; several media sources.
51. Interview with an NGO member, Kaliningrad, 2009.
52. Interview with a member of the Kaliningrad regional Duma, Kaliningrad, 2009.
53. Interview with an NGO member, St Petersburg, 2011.
54. Interview with a member of Kaliningrad regional Duma, Kaliningrad, 2009.
55. Interview with an NGO member, Kaliningrad, 2009.
56. The Commonwealth of Independent States, a regional organization of former Soviet Republics. Today it is a loose association of states which carries more symbolic than formal supranational power, and coordinates cooperation in the fields of trade and

security in particular. For Russia's foreign policy towards the CIS, see, for example, Nygren 2008.

57. Press release of the Russian Ministry of Natural Resources, 10 November 2008, available at: www.mnr.gov.ru/news/detail.php?ID=16945&spetial=Y (accessed 12 December 2013).
58. See *Itar-Tass*, 11 February 2010: 'Sammit deistvii po Baltiiskomu moriu: K itogam vstrechi'.
59. See, for example, *Rossiiskaia Gazeta*, 5 April 2013: 'Severnyi S''ezd; Vystuplenie Ministra inostrannyh del Rossii I.S. Ivanova, 11 June 2003'; see: www.mid.ru/brp_4.nsf/997e7b027bbf661cc3256f6d00540731/ed3f97f16c6576e543256d42002d38fd?Open Document (accessed 12 December 2013); Vystuplenie Ministra Inostrannyh del Rossii C.V. Lavrov na 15-I sessi, 4 June 2009, available at: www.mid.ru/bdomp/ns-dos.nsf/456 82f63b9f5b253432569e7004278c8/432569d800223f34c32575cb0045e08f!OpenDocument (accessed 12 December 2013).
60. *Komsomolskaia Pravda v Kaliningrade*, 12 April 2013: 'Vadim Sidkov: "Evropeitsy bolshe ne schitaiut, chto Baltika – Eto vnutrennee more ES"'.
61. Leonid Korovin, according to *Regnum*, 9 August 2006: 'Vodokanal izbavit stochnye vody iz fosfora za 3–4 goda'.
62. Rasporiazhenie pravitelstva Rossiiskoi Federatsii ot 8 dekabria 2010 g. N 2205-r g. Moskva, available at: www.rg.ru/2010/12/21/mordeyatelnost-site-dok.html (accessed 15 November 2013).
63. Government of the Russian Federation (2001), *Maritime Doctrine of the Russian Federation*, available at: www.scrf.gov.ru/documents/34.html (accessed 15 November 2013).
64. Government of the Russian Federation (2001), *Maritime Doctrine of the Russian Federation*, available at: www.scrf.gov.ru/documents/34.html, p. 10.
65. Rustam Sagitov, Director of the NGO Baltic Sea Foundation, according to *Agenstvo Sotsial'noi Informatsii*, 2 July 2008.
66. *Ekologiia i Zizn*, 31 July 2010: '"Post sdan, post priniat!", ili spasti Baltiku'.
67. For example, *Zelenyi Mir*, 12 November 2010: 'Do 2020 goda Rossiia'.
68. For example, *Rossiiskaia Gazeta*, 5 April 2013: 'Severnyi S''ezd'.
69. Government of the Russian Federation (2010), 'Rabochii den', available at: http://archive.premier.gov.ru/events/news/9375/ (accessed 20 November 2013).
70. Ministry of Foreign Affairs of the Russian Federation (2005), 'Stenogramma Vystuplenia Lavrova', 10 June 2005, available at: www.mid.ru/brp_4.nsf/2fee282eb6df4 0e643256999005e6e8c/f40cd25aa1aa4914c325702000220352?OpenDocument (accessed 20 November 2013).
71. RZD Partner (2006), 'Environmental safety of the port of Primorsk', available at: www.rzd-partner.com/press/289461/ (accessed 9 September 2013).
72. The resolution of the German question took place in December 1972 when the two Germanies and their respective allies recognized each other.
73. On Russia's position in the nitrogen issue at the HELCOM ministerial meeting in 2013, see e.g. a column by Sampsa Vilhunen, the head of the Baltic Sea Programme in WWF Finland, at the website of Centrum Balticum: www.centrumbalticum.org/pulloposti/it%C3%A4meren-suojelu-kompuroi (accessed 20 December 2013_.
74. Ministry of Foreign Affairs of the Russian Federation (2013), *Kontseptsiia vneshnei politiki Rossiiskoi Federatsii* (The Foreign Policy Doctrine of the Russian Federation), available at: www.brunei.mid.ru/doc/kontsep_vneshn_polit_rf.pdf (accessed 12 December 2013).
75. In summertime, dispersed silt from the landfill and port construction site visible in the water gave rise to considerable public concern and criticism (Trumbull 2007, p. 501); these issues were also heatedly discussed in a roundtable that the present author participated in St Petersburg in 2011.
76. See, for example, *Komsomolskaia Pravda v KaliningradeI*, 7 June 2007: 'Musor strashnee globalnogo' potepleniia; *Rossiiskaia Gazeta*, 24 April 2008: 'Ugroza c vozduha'.

77. Between 2006 and 2013, eutrophication (*evtrofikatsiia*) was mentioned in less than ten newspaper articles concerning Baltic Sea cooperation.
78. Personal communication with a former expert of HELCOM, 2013.
79. Nefco (2013), 'The BSAP Fund. Speeding up the ecological restoration of the Baltic Sea', available at: www.nefco.org/sites/nefco.viestinta.org/files/The_BSAP_Fund.pdf (accessed 9 December 2013).
80. Program Implementation Task Force coordinated the implementation of the JCP, the main instrument of HELCOM in the 1990s and early 2000s, during the last years.
81. This list has not been revised, although new hot spots have emerged and several old ones ameliorated.

5. The bilateral case: fisheries management in the Barents Sea

INTRODUCTION

The Barents Sea is home to some of the most productive fishing grounds on the planet, including the world's largest cod stock. Since the 200-mile exclusive economic zones (EEZs) were introduced in the mid-1970s, Norway and the Soviet Union/the Russian Federation have managed the major fish stocks in the Barents Sea together, through the Joint Norwegian-Russian Fisheries Commission. Most importantly, the two parties in 1975 agreed to treat the commercially most important fish stocks in the area – cod and haddock – as shared stocks, dividing the quotas 50/50 between them. At the time of writing (spring 2014), the regime appears to be a successful exception to the rule of failed fisheries management: stocks are in good shape, and institutional cooperation is expanding and takes place in a constructive atmosphere (Hønneland 2012; Stokke 2012). However, that is not to say that the public debate in Russia has not presented different assessments of how the regime works, which is the topic of this chapter.[1]

We focus on four major issues in fisheries relations between Norway and Russia in the post-Soviet period:

- the introduction of the precautionary approach in the late 1990s and the ensuing debates about total allowable catches (TAC);
- enforcement in the Protection Zone around Svalbard after the turn of the millennium;
- discussions on the scientific methods for assessing stock size in the mid-2000s;
- the agreement in 2010 on a delimitation line between the two countries' exclusive economic zones (EEZs).

After a brief overview of the bilateral regime and the jurisdiction of the Barents Sea, these four issue areas are discussed in greater detail. In each section, major events are first presented, and then we turn to the main storylines within the Russian debate. We continue to trace the overarching discourses in which the storylines are situated, before assessing the extent to which actual Russian policy reflects the prevailing discourses.[2]

BACKGROUND

The Bilateral Regime

The Barents Sea (see Figure 5.1) lies north of Norway and northwestern Russia, limited in the north by the Svalbard archipelago and in the east by Novaya Zemlya. The rich fish resources of the Barents Sea have tradition-ally provided the basis for settlement along its shores, especially in north-ern Norway and the Arkhangelsk region of Russia. Since the 1917 Russian Revolution, the city of Murmansk on the Kola Peninsula has been the nerve centre of Russian fisheries in the Barents Sea.

The first steps towards international collaboration in managing the marine resources of the northeast Atlantic came as early as in 1902, with the establishment of the International Council for the Exploration of the Sea (ICES). The European Overfishing Convention of 1946 introduced the first regulatory mechanisms, in the form of minimum mesh size and minimum length of fish brought to land. In 1959, 14 countries, among them Norway and the Soviet Union, signed the North-East Atlantic Fisheries Convention. The mandate of the North-East Atlantic Fisheries Commission (NEAFC) was to provide recommendations on technical regulations, which could be done by simple majority, and fish quotas, which required a two-thirds majority. NEAFC did not succeed in intro-ducing quotas until 1974–75. At the same time, agreement was reached on 200-mile EEZs at the Third UN Conference on the Law of the Sea, and Norway and the Soviet Union began negotiating bilateral management of Barents Sea fish stocks.

When Soviet Minister of Fisheries Aleksandr Ishkov visited Oslo in December 1974, the two countries agreed to establish a joint fisher-ies management arrangement for the Barents Sea.[3] The agreement was signed in Moscow in April 1975 and entered into force immediately. It is a framework agreement, in which the parties state their willingness to work together for the 'protection and rational use of marine living resources' in the NEAFC area. The agreement also established the Joint Norwegian-Soviet (now Norwegian-Russian) Fisheries Commission, which was to meet at least once every year, alternatively on the territory of each party. At the time, the details of the Commission's work were not clear, but when the first session was held in January 1976, the parties agreed to manage jointly the two most important fish stocks in the area, cod and haddock, sharing the quotas 50/50. In 1978, they agreed to treat capelin as a shared stock, and split the quota 60/40 in Norway's favour.[4] When Norway and the Soviet Union declared their EEZs in January and in March 1977, respectively, the bilateral cooperation agreement from 1975 was supplemented by a separate agreement on mutual fishing rights.[5]

During the 1980s, a specific quota exchange scheme developed between the parties, whereby the Soviet Union gave parts of its cod and haddock quotas in exchange for several other species found only in Norwegian waters. These species, especially blue whiting, were found in large quantities but were of little commercial interest to Norwegian fishers. In the Soviet plan economy, volume was more important than (export market) price, so the arrangement was indeed in the mutual interest of both parties.

This changed with the dissolution of the Soviet Union and the introduction of the market economy in Russia. Now cod and haddock, both high-price species on the global fish market, attracted the interest of not only Norwegian but also Russian fishers. Transfers of cod and haddock quota shares from Russia to Norway were reduced, and Russian fishing companies began delivering their catches abroad, primarily in Norway. For the first time, Russian fishers had a real incentive for overfishing their quotas, while Russian enforcement authorities lost control of Russian catches, since quota control had traditionally been exercised at the point of delivery. Norwegian fishery authorities in 1992–93 suspected that the Russian fleet was overfishing its quota, and took steps to calculate total Russian catches, based on landings from Russian vessels in Norway and at-sea inspections by the Norwegian Coast Guard. Norway then claimed that Russia had overfished its quota by more than 50 per cent. The Russian side did not dispute this figure, and the two parties agreed to extend their fisheries' collaboration to include enforcement as well. This involved exchange of catch data, notably the transfer by Norwegian authorities to their Russian counterparts of data on Russian landings of fish in Norway. The successful establishment of enforcement collaboration was followed by extensive coordination of technical regulations, and joint introduction of new measures throughout the 1990s.

Around the turn of the millennium, a new landing pattern emerged. Russian fishing vessels resumed the old Soviet practice of delivering their catches to transport ships at sea. Instead of going to Murmansk with the fish, however, these transport vessels now headed for other European countries: Denmark, the UK, the Netherlands, Spain and Portugal. Norway again took the initiative to assess the possibility of overfishing, but now encountered a less cooperative Russian stance. Thereupon Norway took unilateral measures to calculate overfishing in the Barents Sea, and presented figures that indicated Russian overfishing from 2002, rising to nearly 75 per cent of the total Russian quota in 2005, gradually declining to zero in 2009. The Russian side never accepted these figures, claiming they were deficient at best, and an expression of anti-Russian sentiments at worst. The International Council for the Exploration of the Sea (ICES), however, used them in its estimates of total catches in the Barents Sea during the first decade of the 2000s, thereby providing these figures with a certain level of approval.

A major issue of contention was the setting of quotas in the years around the turn of the millennium, following the introduction of the precautionary approach to fisheries management. We explore this further in the next section.

The Jurisdiction

Agreement on the principle of 200-mile EEZs was reached at the Third UN Conference on the Law of the Sea in 1975. The right and responsibility to manage marine resources within 200 nautical miles of shore was thus transferred to the coastal states at this time. Both Norway and the Soviet Union established their EEZs in 1977 (see Figure 5.1). However, they could not agree on the principle for drawing the delimitation line between their respective zones. The two had been negotiating the delimitation of the Barents Sea continental shelf since the early 1970s, and the division of the EEZs was brought into these discussions. The parties had agreed to use the 1958 Convention of the Continental Shelf as a basis. According to this convention, continental shelves may be divided between states if so agreed. If agreement is not reached, the median line from the mainland border shall normally determine the delimitation line, but special circumstances may warrant adjustments. In the Barents Sea, Norway adhered to the median line principle, whereas the Soviet Union claimed the sector-line principle, according to which the line of delimitation would run along the longitude line from the tip of the mainland border to the North Pole. The Soviets generally held out for the sector-line principle, having claimed sector-line limits to Soviet Arctic waters as early as in 1926. Moreover, they argued that in the Barents Sea special circumstances – notably, the size of the Soviet population in the area, and the strategic significance of the region – made it necessary to deviate from the median line principle.

In 1978, a temporary Grey Zone agreement was reached, to avoid unregulated fishing in the disputed area.[6] This agreement required Norway and the Soviet Union to regulate and control their own fishers and third-country fishers licensed by either of them, and to abstain from interfering in the activities of the other party's vessels or vessels licensed by them. The arrangement was explicitly temporary and subject to annual

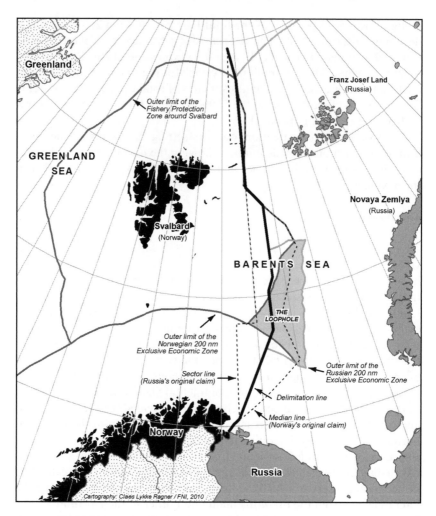

Source: Fridtjof Nansen Institute.

Figure 5.1   Jurisdiction of the Barents Sea

renewal. The Grey Zone functioned well for the purposes of fisheries management,[7] but the prospects of underground hydrocarbon resources in the area pressed the parties to a final delimitation agreement, reached in spring 2010.[8] This recent agreement is a compromise, with the delimitation line midway between the median line and the sector line, as discussed below.

Another area of contention, with more practical implications for fisheries management in the area, is the fishery protection zone around Svalbard. Norway claims the right to establish an EEZ around the archipelago, but has so far refrained from doing so because the other signatories to the 1920 Svalbard Treaty have signalled that they would not accept such a move. The Svalbard Treaty gave Norway sovereignty over the archipelago, which had till then been a no man's land in the European Arctic. However, the treaty contains several limitations on Norway's right to exercise this jurisdiction. Most importantly, all signatory powers enjoy equal rights to let their citizens extract natural resources on Svalbard. Further, the archipelago is not to be used for military purposes, and there are limitations on Norway's right to impose taxes on residents of Svalbard. The original signatories were Denmark, France, Italy, Japan, the Netherlands, Norway, Sweden, the UK and the US. The Soviet Union joined in 1935.

The other signatories (other than Norway) have held that the non-discriminatory code of the Svalbard Treaty must apply also to the ocean area around the archipelago.[9] Other Western countries generally accept that the waters surrounding Svalbard are under Norwegian jurisdiction, but they claim that this jurisdiction must be carried out in accordance with the Svalbard Treaty's non-discriminatory provisions (Pedersen 2008; 2009). Russia, on the other hand, formally considers these waters to be high seas (Vylegzhanin and Zilanov 2007), whereas Norway refers to the treaty text itself, which deals only with the land and territorial waters of Svalbard.

The waters around Svalbard are important feeding grounds for juvenile cod, and the protection zone, determined in 1977, represents a 'middle course' aimed at securing the young fish from unregulated fishing. The protection zone is not recognized by any of the other states that have had quotas in the area since the introduction of the EEZs. To avoid provoking other states, Norway refrained for many years from penalizing violators in the Svalbard Zone. Force was used for the first time in 1993, when Icelandic trawlers and Faroese vessels under flags of convenience – neither with a quota in the Barents Sea – started fishing there. The Norwegian Coast Guard fired warning shots at the ships, which then left the zone. The following year, the first arrest took place in the Svalbard Zone, of an Icelandic vessel fishing without a quota. Sporadic arrests of foreign vessels have followed since then, one of which – the Russian vessel *Chernigov* – will be further discussed below.

THE PRECAUTIONARY APPROACH AND QUOTA SETTLEMENT

Introduction of the Precautionary Approach and Trends in TAC Setting

In the latter half of the 1990s, cod quotas in the Barents Sea were at an all-time high, peaking with a total allowable catch (TAC) of 850 000 tonnes in 1997 – following a gradual increase since the all-time low of 160 000 tonnes in 1990. At the time, marine scientists suspected that their models indicated inflated estimates of stock size, and reduced their estimate of total stock size by 200 000 tonnes. In the following two years, TACs were reduced to 654 000 tonnes and 480 000 tonnes, respectively.

At the same time, the precautionary approach was adopted by both ICES and the Joint Norwegian-Russian Fisheries Commission. The essence of this approach is that lack of scientific knowledge should not be used as a reason for failing to undertake management measures that could prevent the degradation of the environment or the depletion of common pool resources. Whereas it was once considered reasonable to take such measures only when it was established with a high degree of certainty that the environment or resource basis would be seriously threatened without such interference, the introduction of the precautionary approach turned the burden of proof upside down: preventive measures should be postponed or omitted only when there was full scientific certainty that they were *not* necessary.

Despite the significant downward trend in stock size in 1998 and 1999, quotas were still at a reasonable level, as seen from the perspective of the two countries' fishing industries. Then in autumn 1999, ICES sounded the alarm: not only had their models shown inflated estimates of the Barents Sea cod stock, the stock had actually dropped to an alarming level. Spawning stock biomass was believed to be as low as 222 000 tonnes, less than half that prescribed by the precautionary reference point for spawning-stock size defined by ICES. Seen from the outside, if there ever was a time to make use of the precautionary approach, it was now. ICES' primary TAC recommendation for 2000 – intended to restore the spawning stock to acceptable levels within three years – was 110 000 tonnes, nearly five times less than the 1999 quota. However, the Joint Commission arrived at 390 000 tonnes, almost four times above scientific recommendations. The following statement is found in the protocol from this session:

> The Norwegian party notes that the level of the cod quota is alarmingly high in consideration of the available stock assessments and the recommendations from ICES. Taking into account the difficult conditions of the population of

northwestern Russia . . ., Norway has nevertheless found it possible to enter into this agreement.[10]

It was clear that precaution had not prevailed in the joint commission, and that the Norwegian side was disappointed.

The next year, the joint commission made an unexpected move: it established a TAC for the next three years. (Up until then, quotas were set annually.) This quota was slightly above the quota for 2000 (395 000 tonnes) and was to be applied for 2001, 2002 and 2003, unless the stock situation became significantly worse than expected. The three-year element was obviously intended to provide greater predictability. The fishing industries of Norway and Russia were given better opportunities to plan for the immediate future, and those who feared for the health of the cod stock were given assurances that the TAC would not increase even further unless management objectives had been achieved. Judged by the standards of the precautionary approach, however, this left much to be desired. ICES had recommended a TAC of 263 000 tonnes, and in summer 2001 it declared that fishing mortality of the Barents Sea cod stock (natural death plus catch) could have been as high as 0.9 in 2000.[11] Even the most pessimistic estimates during the joint commission's session in November 2000 did not go beyond 0.5.

The new invention announced at the commission's session in 2002 had far wider implications for the further work of the joint commission: a harvest control rule for cod and haddock. The rule consisted of three elements: average fishing mortality should be kept below the precautionary reference point set by ICES for each three-year period; the TAC should not change by more than 10 per cent from one year to the next for cod and 25 per cent for haddock; but, third, exceptions could be made when the spawning stock was below the precautionary reference point. Again we see both biological viability and economic predictability addressed: fishing mortality should be within the precautionary reference point on average for any three-year period, and the fishing industry was secured against large fluctuations in the TAC as long as the spawning stock was above the precautionary reference point. This harvest control rule changed the working form of the commission. Previously, delegation leaders had spent nearly all their time during sessions negotiating the TACs, and agreement was normally reached only at the very end of a session. Now, setting the TAC became more of a technical matter, which could be dealt with sooner rather than later. The harvest control rule was evaluated by ICES in 2005 and found to be in agreement with the precautionary approach.

The cod stock recovered well and the TAC increased gradually, exceeding 600 000 tonnes at the end of the decade. The joint commission stuck to its harvest control rule until 2009, when it decided to increase the cod quota by more than 10 per cent, justifying the move by referring to the satisfactory state of the stock. The spawning stock was actually above one million tonnes at the time.[12] Simultaneously, the commission added to the harvest control rule that fishing mortality should not be *below* 0.30. Implicitly it should be possible to increase the cod TAC by more than 10 per cent if a quota change within 10 per cent would entail fishing mortality below 0.30. In 2010, ICES evaluated the revision of the harvest control rule and deemed it to be precautionary. The same year the joint commission declared that the revised harvest control rule would be used for setting the TAC five years ahead, and then re-evaluated. The cod TAC continued to increase to 724 000 tonnes for 2011 – again an increase beyond 10 per cent, but now in compliance with the revised harvest control rule approved by ICES. For 2013, TAC for the first time exceeded 1 million tonnes.

Storyline: 'It's about time for us to think of the Norwegians as rivals rather than partners'

Behind the formulation in the protocol from the 1999 session in the joint commission (see above), Norway disagreed with the high TAC set for 2000 which lay a hefty disagreement between the two delegations on the interpretation and implications of the scientific advice from ICES. In Norway, the recommended drastic cut in TAC was generally considered legitimate and should be followed up in practice, if not wholeheartedly. The dilemma was seen as one between long- and short-term interests. Should more fish be taken now at the expense of future fisheries, or should less be taken at the expense of today's fishing industry? In Russian fisheries circles, such deliberations were practically absent, at least according to our interview and media data. Instead, Russian discussions centred on the battle of interest between the two states involved, Norway and Russia.

First, the Russian delegation was apparently quite unambiguous in emphasizing at sessions of the joint commission that it was not ready to reduce the year-on-year cod quota any further.[13] As reported by the local media ahead of the session:

> There was a meeting in the regional administration with participants from the fishing industry and scientists from PINRO where ... the tactics and strategy of the Russian party [to the Joint Commission] were discussed. The principle that 'ours' were to follow in the establishment of TACs for cod and haddock was adopted unanimously: not give in [to the Norwegians] on a single kilo.[14]

Second, the Russians seemed to perceive Norway as a rational, unitary actor with mainly economic motives in the establishment of TACs for the joint stocks in the Barents Sea. The Norwegians' insistence on internationally accepted principles for fisheries management, such as sustainability and the precautionary principle, was seen as a smokescreen hiding their real intentions.

> Norway has a very rational administrative system situated in a stable political environment. Before last year's quota negotiations, the Norwegians calculated exactly how large a loss their fishing industry could bear, made plans for compensating losers with revenue from the aqua-culture sector, and decided to go in for a reduction in the cod quota at this level.[15]
>
> Right from the start, the Norwegian delegation pursued a hard line based on ICES' recommendations which, to put it politely, are 'a bit more precautionary than necessary' as far as the assessment of the cod stock is concerned. Here, it should be observed that a range of experts do not exclude the possibility that one of the factors behind the stipulation of these recommendations, with all due respect for this indisputably high respected organization, have been the interests of Norway and the EU countries, whose representatives constitute the majority of the members of ICES' working groups. And it is quite possible that the Norwegian delegation's strong demands for reductions in the cod catches are aimed at maintaining the high price of the country's fish export commodities. . . . This is the third year in a row that the Norwegian party attempts to achieve a reduction in the cod quota, and it is absolutely possible that this insistence is based on the fact that Norway has started artificial breeding of cod. In two to three years' time, the quantity of this fish may reach 180–200,000 tonnes a year, that is, practically equivalent to their share of the quota of 'wild' cod. And in order to maintain the price for the future, they wish to 'freeze' this amount of catch. Whether one likes it or not, the Norwegians at the session [of the Joint Fisheries Commission] gained additional support for their argument by the demands of the 'greens' and parts of the local press.[16]
>
> There is also another reason why the Norwegians went in for the establishment of a fixed cod quota for three years ahead. The Russian participants to the session were told this behind the scenes [of the negotiations]: it is expected that in the course of exactly the next three years Norway will succeed in breeding amounts of cod that, if achieved, will make it possible to reduce the quota of this stock sharply.[17]

Third, there is direct reference by the Russians to (what they perceive as) the decisive economic calculation of Norway as a 'natural' thing. The first quote below is the continuation of the extract above that depicted Norway as using ICES for its own economic motives.

> [I]t is quite possible that the Norwegian delegation's strong demands for reductions in the cod catches have as their objective to maintain the high price of the country's fish export commodities. In principle, there is nothing special about this – every country defends its own interests with the means available to it.[18]
>
> Norway is doing everything it can to destroy the Russian fishing industry. And that's good. That's how it should be. It's just a pity the Russian state isn't strong enough to defend the interests of its inhabitants in the same manner.[19]

Fourth, there is a clear tendency in the Russian press and among actors involved in Russian fisheries to refer to the work of the Russian delegation to the Commission primarily in terms of defending Russia's national interests.

> 'There's a deep misunderstanding that Russia won this year's fishery negotiations in Murmansk,' says [deputy director] Vladimir Torokhov of Sevryba. To the newspaper *Rybnaya Stolitsa* in Murmansk [he] says that, quite the contrary, it was Norway that got its will. 'Our crafty neighbours had right from the start the same quota figures in their heads as the negotiations ended with. . . . We didn't learn the lessons of the previous negotiations and defended our national interests badly'.[20]
>
> Of course, it's necessary to mention the argumentation of the Russian scientists in the negotiations [of the Joint Fisheries Commission], which, to a considerable extent, made possible the achievement of many acceptable results for the members of our northern fishery complex. . . . Our scientists really did a good job at the negotiations.[21]
>
> [In the Joint Fisheries Commission, the Russian scientists] defended the Russian positions in a precise and well-prepared manner.[22]

In conclusion, representatives of the Russian fishing industry and management system appear to agree that the Norwegians should be seen as rivals, not as partners:

> Fishery entrepreneurs and scientists of the Northern basin have held a 'round table' session in Murmansk to work out recommendations for [the] national delegation to future sessions of the Joint Russian-Norwegian Fisheries Commission. 'It's about time for us to think of the Norwegians as rivals rather than partners, in competition for marine bioresources,' said Gennady Stepakhno, head of the Northern Fishery Enterprises Association, at the opening of the meeting. Indeed, it seems to have been the general feeling of the meeting – along with the view that 'there is plenty of fish in the sea, and we must press our demands for an increase in the total allowed catch'.[23]

ENFORCEMENT IN THE SVALBARD ZONE

The Chernigov Episode

The Fishery Protection Zone around Svalbard forms a particular jurisdictional and regulatory complex which, since the turn of the century, has stirred dormant conflicts and exposed differing perspectives between Norwegian and Russian fishery authorities. Hønneland (1998; 1999; 2000; 2012) has shown elsewhere that Norwegian fisheries management in the Svalbard Zone has been relatively successful despite the unclear jurisdictional status of this ocean area. Most of the fishing vessels operating in the zone are Russian.[24] Although Russia has not formally accepted the fishery protection zone, Russian fishers have largely complied with Norwegian fishery regulations in the area and have also followed less formal requests by the Norwegian Coast Guard regarding where to fish in order to avoid excessive intermingling of juvenile fish. Russian vessels do not report to Norwegian fishery authorities about their catches in the zone, and Russian captains refuse to sign inspection forms presented to them by the Norwegian Coast Guard. However, they do welcome Norwegian inspectors on board, and the same inspection procedures are followed in the Svalbard Zone as in the Norwegian EEZ.

To avoid provoking other states, Norway has chosen a 'gentle enforcement' regime in the zone, where violators of fishery regulations are given oral and written warnings, but are not penalized further. Force has been used only against vessels from states that have no quotas in the Barents Sea; see above on the Icelandic fishery in the 1990s.

In the summer of 1998, the Norwegian Coast Guard decided to arrest a Russian vessel for not complying with requests to leave where juvenile fish were overrepresented in the catches. The conflict was solved through diplomatic channels between the two coastal states before the vessel reached the Norwegian port. However, the existing order was seriously challenged when the Norwegian Coast Guard in April 2001 arrested the Russian trawler *Chernigov* in the Svalbard Zone. According to Norwegian authorities, the violations committed by *Chernigov* were exceptionally grave: an extra net had been attached to the trawl whose mesh measured less than half the legal size. Large amounts of juvenile fish were discovered on board at the time of the inspection,[25] and the crew cut the trawl wire in an attempt to avoid discovery of the extra net by the inspectors.[26] 'This is what we define as environmental crime, and that's why we give such a high priority to cases of this sort',[27] explained the chief constable of the Norwegian city of Tromsø after the vessel had been escorted to its port.[28]

Storyline: 'It is always like this: when one state is temporarily weakened, its neighbours will try to take advantage of it'

Russian reactions to the arrest of *Chernigov* were severe. First, an official protest was filed, in which it was argued the arrest had taken place 'in waters where the norms of international law on the high sea apply'.[29] Second, shortly after the arrest, the Russian authorities decided to cease collaboration with Norway in the area of fisheries management. There was a general sentiment in Russian fisheries circles that Norway had broken a 25-year old gentlemen's agreement, whereby Russia accepted Norwegian monitoring of fishing operations in the Svalbard Zone (including physical inspections of Russian vessels), as long as Norway did not behave as if it had formal jurisdiction to do this – for instance, by arresting foreign vessels in the zone. Third, the arrest evoked extraordinarily strong reactions against Norway from Russian politicians at high levels. Most infamous is the statement by Yevgeniy Nazdratenko, leader of the Russian State Committee for Fisheries, that Russian naval vessels should shoot at and sink Norwegian Coast Guard vessels in the Svalbard Zone and do nothing to save their crews.[30] The governor of Murmansk Oblast, Yuriy Yevdokimov, engaged in the debate, commenting on the *Chernigov* incident in the following way: 'In the north, we are facing universal challenges related to the security of Russia. The Norwegians understand this, too. It is always like this: when one state is temporarily weakened, its neighbours will try to take advantage of it.'[31] Finally, the arrest served to bring to the surface what appeared to be suppressed Russian frustrations about what was seen as a gradual expansion of Norwegian control over the Svalbard Zone fisheries. In part, the discourse was linked to similar processes on land on Svalbard, notably the strengthening of Norwegian environmental regulations on the archipelago. The reports below show how this issue was framed before and after the *Chernigov* incident.

There is still disagreement on the Russian–Norwegian fishery in the Svalbard Zone. According to the Paris Convention, signed more than sixty years ago,[32] our country has the right to conduct and expand industrial activity there. However, the Norwegians have recently introduced a range of measures aimed at pressing Russian vessels out of this area.[33]

On 5 June, the Norwegian parliament – the Storting – discussed a new bill on the regulation of environmental affairs on the archipelago of Svalbard. Oslo has also earlier been engaged in environmental protection in the Arctic: large parts of the tundra of Svalbard have been declared nature reserves and national parks, and parts of the ocean areas have been closed for fishing vessels. The new act makes the environmental regulations even stricter – to such an extent that our Ministry of Foreign Affairs found it to be in violation of the old Paris Treaty on Svalbard. More than that: on 6 June, Russia's Deputy Minister of Foreign Affairs, Aleksandr Avdeyev, stated that Norway was 'not far from wanting to establish nature reserves in places where Russian miners either extract coal or have plans to do so' and 'hence force us to leave the island.' . . . After the arrest of the Russian trawler *Chernigov* in this zone, there is sufficient basis to speak about a Norwegian dominance in the zone and discrimination against Russian vessels.[34]

Russia wants extensive changes in the 200-mile fishery protection zone around Svalbard. 'Norway cannot continue to squeeze our fishers out of the area,' says leader of the catch department of the Murmansk-based fishing company AO Sevryba, Vladimir Torokhov. . . . 'The leadership of Sevryba has continuously addressed our State Committee for Fisheries with demands that the Ministry of Foreign Affairs engage in the issue. It is high time the disagreements [between Russia and Norway] are solved.'[35]

METHODS FOR ESTIMATING FISH STOCKS

Schisms in Russian Fisheries Research

The collaboration between Norwegian and Russian marine scientists is often referred to as the core of the bilateral regime. For one thing, the scientific component of the Norwegian-Russian partnership on fisheries management is the one with the longest history.[36] While collaboration on fisheries regulation started in 1975 and on enforcement in 1993, the first steps towards scientific cooperation had been taken as early as in the late nineteenth century (Serebryakov and Solemdal 2002). However, it was only in the 1960s that the Norwegian-Russian/Soviet marine scientific cooperation was formalized (Røttingen et al. 2007).

After the turn of the new millennium, a schism in Russian fisheries science became evident, with attacks by the Russian Federal Research Institute of Marine Fisheries and Oceanography (VNIRO) on ICES and on the regional institute in the Russian northwest, Knipovich Polar Research Institute of Marine Fisheries and Oceanography (PINRO). Russia's regional fisheries research institutes became formally independent of VNIRO in the early 1990s, though their scientific work is still reviewed by the federal institute. At the same time, PINRO's relations with the Norwegian Institute of Marine Research expanded, in line with relaxed East-West relations in the European Arctic more widely – as well as substantial Norwegian funding to support a 'starving' bureaucracy in Russia's northwest. VNIRO had not become part of the international scientific community in ICES to the same extent as PINRO (nor had it received financial support from Norway as the regional institute had) – and now VNIRO scientists began to question the scientific credibility of the models ICES employed in assessing fish stocks of the Barents Sea. The schism is not mentioned in the protocols from the Joint Commission, but complaints by VNIRO scientists about ICES models became 'annual performances' at the plenary sessions of the Commission, as expressed by one member of the Norwegian delegation. At first, VNIRO seemed to lack legitimacy in the Russian delegation, at least in its upper echelons, but Norwegian scientists soon started to fear that VNIRO's approach would actually prevail on the Russian side.

Storyline I: 'The UN fish stocks agreement was written by Greenpeace, with money from the CIA, aimed at destroying the Russian fishing industry'
According to VNIRO, the relationship between recruitment to the stock and the size of the spawning stock was given too much weight

in ICES models; environmental factors such as natural fluctuations caused by swings in temperature and ocean currents were considered to be far more important. Hence, there is no need to be so preoccupied with keeping the spawning stock at a specific level. In the preface to a report from a joint Norwegian-Russian scientific workshop in 2006, VNIRO's director stated: '[the] use of completely unreal models which are based on recruitment dependence on abundance of the spawning stock could be treated as *prophesying voodooism* rather than developing scientifically-based assessments of the state and dynamics of the fish stocks'.[37]

A central point in VNIRO's criticism of ICES is found in the latter's own figures of the catch pressures on (or fishing mortality of) Northeast Arctic cod. Except for a very short period around 1990, fishing mortality has since the 1950s been well above the minimum level that ICES has defined as necessary for securing long-term viability of the stock, i.e. the target reference point. Since the 1970s, fishing mortality has largely been on or above this limit reference point, which according to ICES would represent danger of total collapse of the stock (admittedly, only for one in 20 theoretical runs of the entire existing time series for the stock). The stock has not collapsed. 'If the reference points and ICES models had been correct, there wouldn't have been any fish in the Barents Sea today', one VNIRO scientist noted in an interview.[38] He went on to say: 'The only logical explanation for the divergence between ICES' models and the fact that we still have fish in the Barents Sea is that the estimates are wrong. We underestimate the [cod] stock, and the reason is to be found in the traditional methods.'[39]

Before the interview, the director of the research institute welcomed the interviewers by sighing, 'It's horrible, what's taking place in the Barents Sea at the moment'. This was a usual phrase uttered in the Norwegian fisheries debate at the time: the reference was to the alleged Russian overfishing. However, what the VNIRO director was implying was the exact opposite: he was complaining that the Barents Sea fish stocks were, in his view, *underexploited*. Since ICES models underestimated the stocks, TACs had been set at an artificially low level, to the detriment of the Russian and Norwegian fishing industries. He continued to complain about the recent precautionary norm in international fisheries agreements, which he described as Western inventions aimed at harming the Russian fishing industry, or Russia in general. 'The FAO Fish Stocks Agreement [from 1995, introducing the precautionary principle as the basis for fisheries management] was written by Greenpeace, with money from the CIA, aimed at destroying the Russian fishing industry.'

Storyline II: 'One is amazed at Moscow's lack of logic or sophisticated reasoning'

In a letter dated 13 October 2006, the Russian Federation requested ICES to re-evaluate its northeast Arctic cod assessment in view of new information that had become available since ICES had last evaluated the stock a few months previously.[40] This information included data on Russian transhipments at sea – and the synoptic method for estimating the stock size. A group of scientists from Poland, the Netherlands and France had been appointed for the task, with designated Norwegian and Russian scientists available to assist. According to *ICES Advice 2006*, there was 'good agreement between the reviewers', and they 'supported the ICES June 2006 advice as they did not find the basis for the "new" stock estimate sufficiently strong to reject the [Arctic Fisheries Working Group] assessment'.[41]

The most outspoken criticism, however, came not from Norway nor from ICES, but from VNIRO's own former daughter-institute in Murmansk, PINRO. In their response to a VNIRO report that presented the synoptic method (Borisov et al. 2006), a group of PINRO researchers (Berenboym et al. 2007) more than hinted that VNIRO has promoted the method for financial rather than scientific reasons: 'The alternative method for estimation of stock size has, even if it was conceived by good intentions, in certain cases been used as an instrument to redistribute research quotas within the framework of existing legislature' (ibid. p. 28). The scientific criticism from PINRO is directed mainly at VNIRO's preoccupation with absolute rather than relative figures:

> One has to remind them that what it is important to know, with respect to rational use of a stock, is not the absolute size of the stock, but how it reacts to the intensity of the fishery. It is not so important whether the absolute size of the stock is 1 million or 10 million tonnes – what is important is how the stock reacts to a certain catch under specific conditions. For example, if an annual catch of 800 000 tonnes from a stock of 1 million tonnes makes it possible to maintain a positive tendency in stock dynamics – without displacing the structure of the stock – then such a catch level can be acceptable. And conversely, if a catch of just 100 000 tonnes from a stock of 100 million tonnes leads to a strong displacement in the stock's structure, then one has to consider this catch level as too high. (ibid. p. 27)

The PINRO scientists presented their Moscow colleagues as rank amateurs, incompetent in quantitative analysis:

> Until the authors begin to add maximum values of biomass found for different 'synoptic periods' . . ., it seems as if one can at least observe a simple logic in their reasoning. . . . But when one comes to the addition of the different

maximum biomasses emerging from different time periods, this reminds too much of a pupil's attempts to fit the response to the standard answers in the back of the exercise book. . . . One is amazed at the authors' lack of logic or sophisticated reasoning. (ibid. pp. 25–6)

The regional institute's criticism of its federal mother institute reflects the former's integration with the international, arguably Western-dominated, scientific community. The Moscow-based scientific community is presented as out of sync with international scientific trends: backwards, patriotic and probably corrupt. At a more general level, a PINRO scientist and central figure in the bilateral cooperation with Norway as well as in the multilateral work in ICES, summed up their relations with their foreign colleagues:

We completely share the views held by Norwegian scientists. There is no major disagreement between us. We work together in ICES, we conduct joint scientific expeditions, and we are all behind the stock assessments and quota recommendations that ICES puts forward.[42]

THE 2010 DELIMITATION AGREEMENT

The Agreement

A considerable part of the fishery in the Barents Sea, by Norwegian and Russian vessels, is conducted in the formerly disputed area between the Norwegian and Russian EEZs, where each party controlled their own vessels. After 40 years of negotiation, it came as a surprise when Russian President Dmitri Medvedev and Norwegian Prime Minister Jens Stoltenberg, on 27 April 2010, announced the two countries had reached agreement on the maritime delimitation of the Barents Sea and the Arctic Ocean: the disputed area would be divided into two equal parts. 'We have agreed now on every aspect of this 40-year-old issue: the maritime delimitation line', said Stoltenberg. 'The agreement will be based on international law and the Law of the Sea. It is evenly balanced, and will serve both countries.' He continued: 'The essence of our policy, is not speed racing, but cooperation and mutual achievement, and today our two nations have reached an understanding in this regard.' To this, Medvedev added: 'This has been a difficult issue and made cooperation between our countries difficult. Today we have reached agreement. We need to live with our neighbours in friendship and cooperation. Unresolved issues are always a source of tension.' How had they had managed to keep news of the delimitation treaty secret, Medvedev was asked. To this, he parried: 'In Russia, as you know, the conspiracy traditions are deep-rooted [*laughter*] and well-practised. I don't know about Norway.'[43]

The joint statement, signed by Foreign Ministers Sergei Lavrov and Jonas Gahr Støre the same day, details the process involved in determining the outer limits of the continental shelf.

> As stated in the Ilulissat Declaration of the coastal States around the Arctic Ocean of 28 May 2008, both Norway and the Russian Federation are committed to the extensive legal framework applicable to the Arctic Ocean, as well as to the orderly settlement of any possible overlapping claims.
>
> Bearing in mind the developments in the Arctic Ocean and the role of our two States in this region, they highlight the bilateral cooperation with regard to the determination of the outer limits of the continental shelf, in accordance with the United Nations Convention on the Law of the Sea.[44]

On 15 September 2010, the Treaty on the Maritime Delimitation and Cooperation in the Barents Sea and Arctic Ocean was duly signed in Murmansk by Lavrov and Støre, in the presence of Medvedev and Stoltenberg, and entered in force on 7 July 2011.[45] This was a compromise that divided the disputed area into two equal parts while also establishing a single common boundary to the continental shelf and economic zones. It consists of three parts: the border agreement and two annexes on fisheries and 'Transboundary Hydrocarbon Deposits', both of which are integral parts of the treaty. The fisheries appendix broadly commits the parties to the continuance of the Joint Norwegian-Russian Joint Fisheries Commission. On a more specific note, the 1975 agreement between Norway and USSR on cooperation in the fishing industry, and the 1976 agreement concerning mutual relations in the field of fisheries, will remain in force for 15 years after the entry into force of the new delimitation treaty. At the end of that period, both agreements will remain in force for successive six-year terms, unless one of the parties notifies the other at least six months before the expiry of the six-year term of its intention to terminate one or both of them. In the previously disputed area within 200 nautical miles from the Norwegian or Russian mainland, the technical regulations concerning, in particular, mesh and minimum catch size, set by each of the parties for their fishing vessels, will continue to apply for a transitional period of two years from the treaty's entry into force. The appendix concerning transboundary hydrocarbon deposits provides instructions for what 'unitization in the exploitation of transboundary hydrocarbon deposits' whereby such deposits are to be exploited as a unit in a way agreed on by both parties.

Storyline I: 'The agreement is greeted in Norway as a huge victory over Russia'

Hailed by Norwegians as a great example of what friends can achieve when they put their heads together to reach a compromise that protects the interests of both, the delimitation treaty was not greeted with the same unqualified enthusiasm in Russia. The very day the agreement was signed, the media in northwest Russia unleashed a campaign reminiscent of the one it had run 11 years earlier in response to the setting of catch quotas ('we haven't a fish to give away'). 'Today', declared the title of a September 2010 article from the news agency Regnum, 'Russia is giving Norway a chunk of the Barents Sea.'[46] 'It would be interesting to know', the agency's otherwise unidentified 'expert', Nikolay Bogdanov, says,

> ... under what circumstances and commitments and to whom (!?)[47] the [Norwegians] compelled the diplomatic corps and government of Russia to get involved in a blitz war by signing ... the agreement on the border in the area called 'grey' by the Norwegian delegation in 1974, that is, the disputed zone in the Barents Sea, in April 2010. The loss of the oil and gas deposits in the shelf which has now been ceded to Norway means a loss to coming generations of Russians of up to 5 billion tonnes of recoverable oil equivalents. And Russian fishermen stand to lose about 150 000 tonnes per annum, mainly species of cod.

In its September 2010 edition, *Argumenty i fakty* fired off the following salvo: 'Right up to the last minute, Norway did not believe the agreement would be signed, but Russia took this step which today is being described as a gigantic capitulation, even indeed an act of treachery.'[48] Like so many others, Vasily Nikitin, Director-General of the Union of Fishermen of the North, drew attention to the old Soviet sector declaration from 1926 to explain the actual meaning of jurisdiction in the Barents Sea. The old declaration had still 'not been formally revoked', he noted, but with the treaty in hand the Norwegians now have all the 'leverage' they want to run Russian fishermen off the most abundant fishing grounds in the Barents Sea. Referring to the idea that the Russian fleet will never be able to meet the stringent Norwegian requirements, he concludes in some style, 'They will say to us: "We're not throwing you out, you've just got to be tall, well-built and fair-haired!"'[49] – no place for short, dark Mongols here, in other words.

'They'll elbow us out eventually', predicted the headline of an article in the business paper *Vzglyad* one month after the agreement was signed.[50] 'We've lost 90 000 square kilometres and the opportunity to fish in the western parts of the Barents Sea', declared Vyacheslav Zilanov, deputy head of the Russian Fisheries Agency's public chamber, and vice-president of the All-Russian Association of Fishing Enterprises and Fish Exporters (VARPE). Zilanov was incensed at Russia's surrender of half of the previously disputed area with Norway and concerned about the resultant huge losses to the Russian fishing industry. While an average of between 210 000 and 215 000 tonnes are fished annually in the area east of the dividing line, some 300 000 to 315 000 tonnes are taken in the area to the west. Moreover, Zilanov protested, the waters around Svalbard – under the terms of the delimitation agreement – are all under Norwegian jurisdiction. 'We have lost territory, 60 000 to 90 000 square kilometres. We have lost the chance of fishing in the whole of the western Barents Sea – if not today, then tomorrow. They're going to force us out. It will be the end.'[51]

> **Interviewer**: Did I understand you properly [when you said] the Svalbard Treaty is still in force, and only Norway can specify the fishery rules? That's to say, the Norwegians can easily 'throttle' our fisheries by, for example, banning 'outdated' fishing methods used by our Russian fishermen?
> **Zilanov**: We don't use 'outdated' methods. We use different methods to catch ground fish and pelagic fish in the Barents Sea: bottom and pelagic trawls, long lines and nets. The fisheries of Russia and Norway are asymmetric. What does that mean? Russia catches 95 per cent of its fish with bottom trawls and 5 per cent by line. The Norwegians use lines to catch 70 per cent; trawling accounts for only 30 per cent. So of course the Norwegians can introduce new rules on trawlers and say 'this isn't discriminatory because they apply to Norwegian fishermen as well'. But our fishing fleet will bear the brunt. That was the first example. Example number two: Norway could ban bottom trawls in its waters. That would be the end of the Russian fisheries. . . .
> **Interviewer**: The agreement is greeted in Norway as a huge victory over Russia. Do you have any comments?
> **Zilanov**: I wouldn't put it like that, that Norway has triumphed over Russia. We're not an easily vanquished country. Let me put it like this. What Norway has done in the negotiations with the Russian Foreign Ministry is a glittering diplomatic, political and economic achievement. . . .

Criticism of the treaty was not a flash in the pan; it rumbled on and effectively delayed Russian ratification. The complaints were repeated in an open letter to the Foreign Minister Lavrov on 17 May 2010, and to President Medvedev on 8 September 2010. 'The coastal population in Russia's regions', warned the writers of the letter to Medvedev, 'will suffer harshly, socially and economically', unless something can be done to renegotiate the deal so that the interests of Russian fishermen are better protected. 'Revered Dmitry Anatolyevich, do not forget the astute saying "measure seven times, cut once", nor the first commandment of our fishing fleet captains: "danger is never far away".'[52]

Storyline II: 'The Barents Sea is our common kitchen garden'

But there is a competing image of Norway's intentions in the Barents Sea. In an article entitled 'This is Russia and Norway's promising kitchen garden',[53] former governor of Murmansk oblast, Yuri Yevdokimov, paints a rather sympathetic picture of Norwegian-Russian relations in the Barents Sea. 'Now that Russia and Norway are doing such a lot of things together, like extracting deposits in the Shtokman field and the global nuclear safety measures, God has commanded us to get rid of the inconsistencies in the Grey Zone.' ('Grey Zone' is used incorrectly here for the disputed area: the two are not wholly co-extensive.) While acknowledging that he is not appraised of the details of the agreement and the impact they will have, he says he is confident that Russian negotiators have done what they can to defend Russian interests in the best possible way. Asked by a journalist whether Russia might not have got a better deal if they had played on the fact that Norway has practically run out of oil, Yevdokimov replied:

> No, that's not how I see it. The Norwegians are our neighbours – indeed, our very good neighbours – even if they do belong to a different defence alliance. They have extensive experience of working on the shelf. They have the gear and the technology. We don't. The sooner we can benefit from their lead, the better it will be for both countries. Apart from that, it was important for Russia and Norway to reach an agreement at this point in time. Many countries are looking at the disputed areas of the shelf, even countries with no connections to the sea. Everyone has something they would like to do there. In reality, the Barents Sea is our common kitchen garden, useful today and promising for the future, because we are the only ones who border these immensely prolific waters. Now we have agreed that we alone can operate like rulers here, and we alone who set the rules of the game.

Mikhail Nenashev, member of the State Duma for Murmansk oblast and member of Medvedev's team on the trip to Oslo, likewise sees the agreement as having 'a huge impact on our country'.[54] He places the deal in a wider Arctic context, and is even clearer on what Russia should expect to get from Norway in return for the treaty: not only support to ensure that the principles of the Law of the Sea are applicable in the Arctic – he also sees the Norwegian and Russian submissions to the Continental Shelf Commission as part and parcel of the same undertaking.

> **Interviewer**: Our job is to win the whole Arctic. Is the agreement with Norway likely to hasten progress and strengthen our influence over other sectors in the Arctic region?
> **Petrovich**: We are entitled to expect the same measure of indulgence from Norway. We didn't interfere when they submitted their claims concerning the shelf. And since we have declared our willingness to resolve boundary issues in

the spirit of good neighbourliness, we are entitled to expect Norway to support our claim in return. Of course, we will keep a close eye on how Norway behaves in this issue.

In October 2010, the Murmansk regional Duma committee on Natural Resources and Agriculture adopted a resolution urging the State Duma and Federation Council not to ratify the delimitation treaty.[55] In the Regional Duma itself, the proposal also won a majority – but not unanimity. The declaration was quietly withdrawn a month later 'without explanation', according to *NordNews*.[56] In a long interview with *Murmansky vestnik*, Evgeny Nikora, then Speaker of the Murmansk Regional Duma, his deputy and United Russia faction leader, Igor Saburov, and Andrei Ivanov, chair of the Committee on Natural Resources and Agriculture, are lavish in their praise of the boundary agreement.[57] 'Two months have passed', the article begins, since the agreement was signed. 'Passions have died down, and we can reflect more deeply about what the deal can give us, after all.' 'The agreement', says the Speaker, 'is historic in character'; a 'serious step in a positive direction [and] a new platform for cooperation', his deputy adds. Nevertheless, says Igor Saburov, while the Russians need to keep a close eye on how the Norwegians behave, 'we should not anticipate anything untoward. Last month's resolution by the Regional Duma was premature. Further delays in ratification would only give the Norwegians "unhealthy food" to bring up in the talks ahead'. Let's see how the agreement works in practice before we do anything, is the advice. The chair of the Committee on Natural Resources and Agriculture explains why he changed his mind:

Having had several important meetings in Moscow, I came to the conclusion that fishing is not the most important thing in this respect, not by a long way. The big issue is the division of the Arctic shelf; the 'race for the Arctic' has a lot of competitors already. We also need to remember the implications on the strategic national interests of the whole country, and our children and grandchildren will hopefully be grateful for the decisions we make today. The agreement will, of course, be ratified, but the work of correcting it is already in progress. We and Norway 'breathe in sync' in many areas. We understand each other, just as the residents of the [Soviet] *kommunalki* [council tenements where several families shared the same kitchen and bathroom] would argue and then make up again. If a broken gas valve needed replacing, they worked together – because if the flap fell out, none of them would be safe. I don't think we should worry too much whether the Norwegians are going to institute particularly Draconian measures. They are a reasonable people and would never do anything like that.

EMERGING DISCOURSES

We see reflected above rather similar views on the Norwegian-Russian interface in the Barents Sea, whether TAC settlement, enforcement, fisheries science or jurisdiction is at issue – and over time from the late 1990s to the delimitation agreement in 2010. The constant factor is not so much regulatory technicalities or biological viability of the fish stocks, but *Russia's place in the world* and *the rules of the game in international politics.* Is the West – in this case, Norway – in constant pursuit of inflicting harm on Russia? Or is it a reliable collaboration partner?

The Zero-Sum Game Discourse, Malign Version

A red thread in the stories told above about major events in Norwegian-Russian fishery relations is the Russian assumption that Norway's underlying motive in its dealings with Russia is to inflict as much harm as possible on its eastern neighbour. Along with this comes self-criticism of Russian naïveté: 'Oh, us Russians – we think too well of people, and once again we find ourselves encircled by those shrewd Westerners.' In discussions about quota levels around the turn of the century, the head of the major fisheries association in Murmansk concluded, 'it's about time for us to think of the Norwegians as rivals rather than as partners'. During the 1990s, the Norwegians had led the way in the bilateral fisheries regime, and too late the Russians understood that the Norwegian motive was to suddenly cut the Barents Sea cod quotas in order to pave the way for artificially bred Norwegian cod onto the world market. To achieve this aim, the Norwegians had ensured support from their Western allies in ICES, according to public opinion in Russia. At around the same time, Norway conducted the first arrest of a Russian fishing vessel in the Svalbard Zone and introduced a new environmental act on Svalbard that significantly curbed planned Russian mining activities. The assumption was that Norway was taking the opportunity, now that the Soviet Union was dismantled and the new Russian Federation was economically devastated, to sweep the Russians out of Svalbard and the Barents Sea once and for all. In discussions about scientific methods for estimating fish stocks, it was argued that precaution in fisheries management was actually a Western invention – even sponsored by the CIA – intended to ruin the Russian economy even further. And if the 2010 delimitation agreement in the Barents Sea was a compromise to the benefit of both parties, why then was it 'greeted in Norway as a huge victory over Russia'? Again, this was an instance of Western shrewdness: the Norwegians had planned it all years in advance and now seized the moment when Russia needed allies in its battle with Canada over the Arctic shelf. With the delimitation line in place, however, Norway has all the necessary leverage for elbowing the Russians out of the Svalbard zone for good, as by introducing new requirements to fishing gear too expensive for the Russian fleet to purchase: 'We're not throwing you out, you've just got to be tall, well-built and fair-haired.'

Interestingly, however, the Norwegians are not scolded – quite the contrary, they are put forward as ideals to strive for: 'Norway does everything it can to destroy the Russian fishing industry – and that's good, that's how it should be.' It is Russians' lack of similar shrewdness that is deplored: 'It's just a pity that the Russian state isn't strong enough to defend the interests of its inhabitants in the same manner.' Things are indeed as they should be: 'It is always like this: when one state is temporarily weakened, its neighbours will try to take advantage of this.' It is even in the interest of one state to reduce its own good (as Norway was allegedly ready to do in the 1999 TAC setting), as long as the opponent loses even more. Moreover: 'there is nothing special about this: every country defends its own interests with the means available to it.' International politics is a zero-sum game; states are in constant pursuit of political and economic goods at the expense of other states. This is something similar to a natural law – observable, stable, predictable and nothing to go crazy over.

The Zero-Sum Game Discourse, Benign Version

We also see traces of a more benign variant of the zero-sum game discourse. Yes, Norway is trying to maximize its own material interest, preferably at the expense of Russian interests – but not necessarily so, and not at any cost. The Barents Sea is 'our common kitchen garden', says former Murmansk governor Yevdokimov, adding that God himself has commanded us to overcome disagreements about a delimitation line. But we should not forget that this is the same man who stated that any country would take advantage of its neighbour as soon as the latter is temporarily weakened. And even when speaking about the joint kitchen garden, he takes care to remind us that Norway belongs to a different defence alliance. In a similar vein, State Duma Deputy Nenashev speaks of the delimitation agreement as a fair barter deal, but one that Russians cannot completely rely on Norway to comply with: 'we will keep a close eye on how Norway behaves'. Likewise, United Russia faction leader Saburov in the Murmansk regional Duma declares that Russia 'should not anticipate anything untoward' from Norway, but will have to monitor its Western neighbour's actions closely. States are strongly oriented towards self-interest, and the behaviour of other states should be kept a close eye on – you cannot really trust anyone, but still there is some variance in how states really behave. It is not taken for granted that states will be willing to reduce their own good as long as other states lose even more. Zero-sum thinking is still a tendency in international relations, but not necessarily a natural law.

The Joint Benefits Discourse

In general, the Barents Sea fisheries have attracted the interest of the Russian public – the media, politicians and interest groups – only when some level of conflict arises: when there is sharp disagreement about quotas, when Norway arrests Russian vessels in the disputed Svalbard Zone, or when Moscow scientists suddenly come up with models sharply at odds with the internationally accepted norms for stock assessment. One might say that it is not very surprising therefore, that disagreement between the two states should come to dominate the national Russian discourse. Nevertheless, comparison with the Norwegian public discourse surrounding the same events (Hønneland 2003; 2006; 2012) shows that the zero-sum game discourse is not the only possible way of framing these issues. Whereas the Russian discourse focuses on national interest, viewing Norwegian-Russian fishery relations as a zero-sum national battle, the Norwegian discourse revolves around mutual benefits for the two countries, with short-term economic benefits versus long-term sustainability as the main issue for debate (see Hønneland 2003). Are any traces of such a 'joint benefit discourse' visible on the Russian side?

For one thing, there is a sliding passage between the benign version of the zero-sum game discourse and a more pure joint-benefit discourse. We saw above that regional politicians in Murmansk speak of the Barents Sea as 'our common kitchen garden' and the delimitation agreement as a fair deal. Nevertheless, they continue to refer to Norway as a potentially unreliable partner which has to be watched every step of the way, inherently inclined to sacrifice international obligations once the opportunity arises. On the other hand, also speaking in the aftermath of the regional Duma's withdrawal of its 'protest' of the delimitation agreement, the head of the Committee on Natural Resources and Agriculture downplays the competitive element of Norwegian-Russian relations. The two neighbours, he says, 'breathe in sync', 'understand each other just like the residents of the [Soviet] *kommunalki*'; they can quarrel and make up, but would never institute 'particularly draconian measures' towards each other.

We find another expression of a joint-benefit discourse in how Russian scientists present their dealings with the outside world, with Norwegian colleagues in the bilateral regime and the wider European scientific community in ICES: 'We completely share . . . views'; there is 'no major disagreement'; 'conduct joint scientific expeditions'; and 'are all behind the stock assessments and quota recommendations that ICES puts forward'. The good relations between PINRO and international scientific communities are even more strongly, albeit implicitly, expressed in PINRO scientists' harsh scolding of their VNIRO colleagues. Admittedly, these statements in isolation say no more than 'cooperation is going on and functions well'. If nothing else, they at least seem to reflect the absence of zero-sum thinking in these circles. Cooperation between scientists from all countries around the northeast Atlantic is necessary to map the entire ocean area. The agreement on joint methods strengthens the scientific quality of the data and ensuing quota recommendations, as do the established peer-review processes within ICES, whereby Barents Sea data from Norwegian and Russian scientists are critically scrutinized by scientists from other countries.

CONCLUSIONS

Now let us return to how Russia has in fact behaved in the Joint Norwegian-Russian Fisheries Commission. The Russians refused to give in to Norwegian demands of quota cuts in 1999, but then compromised on a three-year quota in 2000 and a harvest control rule in 2002, bringing quota levels in the Barents Sea into line with precautionary requirements defined by ICES. Russia protested the Norwegian arrest of the trawler *Chernigov* in the Svalbard Zone in 2001, but soon resumed amicable fisheries relations with Norway, and towards the end of the decade no longer protested Norwegian arrests in the area. The alternative methods for estimating stock size proposed by VNIRO were rejected by both PINRO and ICES, and in the joint commission the Russian side never put much effort into convincing the Norwegians to adopt the new methods. The delimitation agreement was signed by Russia: moreover, it was defended by the higher political echelons in the country when criticism began to surface.

The zero-sum game discourse is mainly reflected in statements by the region's fishing industry, regional media (fishery newspapers in particular) and long-timers in the Russian fisheries bureaucracy. One example of the latter category is Vyacheslav Zilanov, whose criticism of the delimitation agreement was noted above. Zilanov wears many hats in the Russian fishery complex; according to the above-mentioned article he is currently deputy head of the Federal Fisheries Agency's public chamber and vice-president of the union for employees in the fisheries sector, VARPE. Russian media have also described him recently as representing the governor in Murmansk in fishery issues, and as chairman of the board of fishing companies. In the 1990s, he was fisheries adviser in the Russian Parliament, and in Soviet times Deputy Minister for the Fishing Industry – and head of the Soviet delegation to the Joint Norwegian-Soviet Fisheries Commission. Frequently claiming himself to be a 'friend of Norway', he has for many years been a fervent critic of the Russian authorities' weakness in fisheries relations with Norway. In the aftermath of the delimitation agreement, he stood forth as the leading figure in the internal Russian criticism (Hønneland 2014).

In general, the representatives of the malign version of the zero-sum game discourse emerge as critics, not definers of Russian politics in the interface with Norway. There is one important exception: the commission's session in 1999, when negotiations were broken for several days and the Norwegians finally had to give in and accept a TAC four times higher than ICES' scientific recommendation. Interestingly, the Russian delegation was that year dominated by regional actors from the fishing industry. The next year (following Putin's entry as president – coincidental?), Moscow was again in control, and a decade of Russian willingness to compromise with Norway followed. The delimitation agreement in 2010 crowned the decade of success by the compromise *per se*. One of Zilanov's complaints about the agreement was that 'experts' – people with experience from the fishing industry – were expelled from the Russian delegation in the final rounds of the delimitation negotiations when compromise was effectively reached. To conclude, then, the malign version of the zero-sum game discourse – concentrated mainly in the country's traditional fishery complex – has reflected Russian opposition, but only to a small extent defined actual politics in relation to Norway in the Barents Sea.

PINRO scientists are the primary representatives of the joint-benefits discourse, situated as they are in an internationalized scientific community. Their influence on Russian politics has largely been indirect, since ICES advice has been followed by the joint commission since the turn of the century. The most influential discourse seems to be the benign version of the zero-sum game discourse, whereby Russia is seen as a player in an international game between states ready to seek *ad hoc* compromise whenever they see it as in their interest, but not necessarily willing to reduce their own good as long as other states lose even more (as presupposed by the malign version of the zero-sum discourse). The Russian authorities have openly defended the delimitation agreement with Norway as a step on the way to control of the Arctic shelf; with another Arctic state (Norway) even more closely attached, they stand stronger *vis-à-vis* their main opponent, Canada. In fisheries management *per se*, no justifications for the compromises with Norway are given, other than reference to the fact that the two countries show their ability to manage the Barents Sea fish stocks sustainably, to the economic benefit of both.

In sum, the Norwegian-Russian interface in the Barents Sea is to some extent a genuinely *environmental* encounter. Both states have taken the task of sustainable fisheries management seriously, and the bilateral management regime stands out as an example for emulation in international fisheries politics. But it is also a marketplace where Russia can trade fish – or jurisdiction – for other goods, such as political support from Norway on other political issues, as in the delimitation negotiations. Furthermore, it is an arena where Russia can display itself as a 'civilized' partner in international politics more widely: Russia follows scientific advice in fisheries management; Russia abides by its international obligations; Russia collaborates peacefully with a Western neighbour; Russia is willing to compromise. To a large extent, Russian behaviour in the Joint Norwegian-Russian Fisheries Commission is a reflection of which internal actors are most influential. At the 1999 session, regional industry actors were in the lead, and their 'malign' zero-sum thinking prevailed and dictated quota settlement, much to the dismay of Norway. After the turn of the millennium, high-ranking civil servants from Moscow took over; in the delimitation agreements the Ministry of Foreign Affairs was at the helm, while representatives from the fishery complex were ousted from the Russian delegation in the final rounds. The result was a relaxed collaborative atmosphere and substantial compromise, which better suited the Norwegian position of including elements of genuine environmental concern (see Hønneland 2003; 2012).

To the extent that Russia intends to pursue sustainable fisheries management and show to the world that it is a reliable cooperation partner in international politics, these objectives are achieved simultaneously. The dominant compromise-oriented practice does not reflect the prevailing zero-sum discourse. On the other hand, this discourse delayed Russian ratification of the delimitation agreement; it led to unsustainable quota levels at the beginning of the new millennium; and it is reflected in internal Russian quarrels about scientific methods for fish stock assessment. When analysing Russia, we must recognize the Norwegian-Russian fisheries interface as an encounter not only between different states, but between different Russian positions, material as well as discursive.

NOTES

1. For an analysis of the Norwegian position/approach/discourses to the regime, see Hønneland (2003).

2. The empirical presentation builds mainly Russian media articles and partly on interviews carried out from 1994 to 2012 by Geir Hønneland with members of the Russian fishery complex, in particular for his anniversary publication for the Joint Commission to its 30th anniversary (Hønneland 2006), for a research project on knowledge disputes in Russian fisheries science (Aasjord and Hønneland 2008), and post-agreement bargaining in the Barents Sea (Hønneland 2012). Sources are indicated only for direct citations and data obtained from other sources than protocols and observation.

3. 'Avtale mellom Regjeringen i Unionen av Sovjetiske Sosialistiske Republikker og Regjeringen i Kongeriket Norge om samarbeid innen fiskerinæringen', in (1975) *Overenskomster med fremmede stater*, Oslo: Ministry of Foreign Affairs, pp. 546–9.

4. Norway originally demanded a higher share of cod and haddock since more of these stocks are found in Norwegian than in the Soviet/Russian zone, but accepted a 50/50 split presumably because the difference in distribution was not overwhelming – and the Soviet Union was, after all, a superpower. However, the Soviets did accept a larger share of capelin for the Norwegians, probably because the difference in distribution between the two countries' zones is higher for capelin than for cod and haddock, and because capelin is a less significant stock in terms of value and volume.

5. 'Avtale mellom Regjeringen i Kongeriket Norge og Regjeringen i Unionen av Sovjetiske Sosialistiske Republikker om gjensidige fiskeriforbindelser', in (1977) *Overenskomster med fremmede stater*, Oslo: Ministry of Foreign Affairs, pp. 974–8.

6. 'Avtale mellom Norge og Sovjetunionen om en midlertidig praktisk ordning for fisket i et tilstøtende område i Barentshavet med tilhørende protokoll og erklæring', in (1978) *Overenskomster med fremmede stater*, Oslo: Ministry of Foreign Affairs, p. 436.

7. That is to say, there was not much dispute between Norway and the Soviet Union/ Russia as to how enforcement should be conducted in the Grey Zone. To the extent that there was Russian overfishing in the Barents Sea, however, it was problematic that the entire area covered by the Grey Zone was inaccessible to the Norwegian Coast Guard.

8. Treaty between Norway and the Russian Federation concerning 'Maritime Delimitation and Cooperation in the Barents Sea and the Arctic Ocean', available at: www.regjeringen.no/upload/UD/Vedlegg/Folkerett/avtale_engelsk.pdf (accessed 5 June 2014).

9. The strongest opposition to the protection zone has come from the UK. The US, Germany and France have formally just reserved their position, which implies that they are still considering their views. Finland declared its support to the protection zone in 1976, but has not repeated it since then. Canada expressed its support to the Norwegian position in a bilateral fisheries agreement in 1995, but this agreement has not entered into force.

10. (1999) *Protokoll for den 28. sesjon i Den blandete norsk-russiske fiskerikommisjon*, Oslo: Ministry of Fisheries, Art. 5.1.

11. *Nordlys*, 6 June 2001.

12. (2010) *ICES Advice 2010. Book 3: The Barents and the Norwegian Sea*, Copenhagen: International Council for the Exploration of the Sea, p. 6. Spawning-stock biomass had been above the target reference point (460 000 tonnes) since 2002. Fishing mortality had been reduced from well above the limit reference point (0.74) around the turn of the millennium to well below the target reference point (0.40) since 2006.

13. There have been no signs in official statements, in the press or in Geir Hønneland's numerous interviews with actors within the Russian fisheries sector, of divergent opinions within the Russian delegation to the joint fisheries commission. As far as the Russian population at large is concerned, it is naturally impossible to exclude that there are people sympathetic to the Norwegian position, but Geir Hønneland has been unable to find representatives of this view during his interviews with fisheries representatives in Russia or in written material.

14. *Rybnaya stolitsa*, 15 November 1999.

15. Interview with Russian bureaucrat, Murmansk, February 2000.

16. *Rybatskiye novosti*, No. 3–4, 2001.

17. *Rybnyy biznes*, November 2000.

18. *Rybatskiye novosti*, No. 3–4, 2001.
19. Interview with Murmansk resident, April 2001.
20. *Fiskeribladet*, 14 December 1999.
21. *Rybnyy biznes*, November 2000.
22. Vice-Governor of Murmansk Oblast to *Murmanskiy vestnik*, November 2000.
23. IntraFish, www.intrafish.com, 2 November 2001 (accessed 3 November 2001).
24. This can be explained by the fact that Norway allocates approximately 75 per cent of its cod quota in the Barents Sea to coastal vessels operating closer to the Norwegian mainland, whereas the Russian fleet consists almost exclusively of ocean-going trawlers – see discussion above on conflicts of interest within the Norwegian fishing industry.
25. Aftenposten Interaktiv, www.aftenposten.no, 22 April 2001 (accessed 22 April 2001).
26. CNN Norge, www.cnn.no, 25 April 2001 (accessed 25 April 2001). The Norwegian Coast Guard succeeded in 'catching' the net so as to secure evidence of the crime.
27. Aftenposten Interaktiv, www.aftenposten.no, 22 April 2001 (accessed 22 April 2001).
28. The next time Norway attempted to arrest a Russian vessel in the Svalbard Zone was in 2005 – again, for serious violations of fishing regulations, including overfishing. Again the arrest was not carried through, but the reason was different than in the 1998 incident: the captain of the Russian fishing vessel changed course abruptly and escaped to a Russian harbour – taking along the Norwegian inspectors who were still on board. He was later sentenced in a Russian court, and official Russian reactions to the Norwegian move were much milder than in 2001. In 2009–10, the Norwegian Coast Guard carried out a handful of arrests of Russian fishing vessels in the protection zone around Svalbard, without formal reactions from the Russian authorities.
29. Aftenposten Interaktiv, www.aftenposten.no, 23 April 2001.
30. *Fiskeribladet*, 28 September 2001.
31. *Nordlys*, 12 June 2001.
32. When this was written, the Svalbard Treaty had actually been signed more than 80 years ago.
33. *Rybnaya stolitsa*, No. 39, 2000.
34. *Rybnaya stolitsa*, No. 24, 2001.
35. *Fiskeribladet*, 17 October 2000.
36. See Jakobsen and Ozhigin (2011) for an overview of Norwegian–Russian fisheries research cooperation.
37. (2006) *On Necessity of Improvement of the Russian–Norwegian Management Strategy for Cod in the Fisheries in the Barents Sea*, Workshop for Discussion of the Joint Management of the Barents Sea Cod Stock, Nor-Fishing 2006, Moscow: VNIRO Publishing, p. 4 (emphasis added).
38. Interview in Moscow, December 2007.
39. Ibid.
40. (2006) *ICES Advice 2006. Book 3: The Barents and the Norwegian Seas*, Copenhagen: International Council for the Exploration of the Sea, p. 28.
41. Ibid.
42. Interview with Russian scientist, Murmansk, October 2000.
43. nrk.no, 27 April 2010 (accessed 27 April 2010).
44. 'Joint Statement on Maritime Delimitation and Cooperation in the Barents Sea and the Arctic Ocean', press release, Norwegian Foreign Ministry, 27 April 2010, available at: www.regjeringen.no (accessed 10 July 2013).
45. For a detailed examination, see Jensen (2011).
46. *Regnum*, 15 September 2010.
47. Punctuation as in original.
48. *Argumenty i fakty*, 22 September 2010.
49. *Regnum*, 28 October 2010. *Vysokij strojnyj blondin* is translated rather broadly as 'tall, strapping blonds' by Århus (2012). *Blondin* is the masculine form of the noun derived from the adjective 'blond' (the feminine form is *blondinka*). While Århus's variant is flamboyant, the present authors have opted for a more literal translation.

50.   *Vzgljad*, 27 October 2010.
51.   Hønneland (2014) argues at length that the delimitation treaty does not influence Norway's alleged interest in or potential for forcing the Russians out of the Barents Sea. If Norway had wanted to ban Russians from the Norwegian zone or the Svalbard Zone, or outlaw bottom trawling, it could have done both prior to and after the delimitation came into effect, but it simply has no interest in doing so. In brief, it is in Norway's interest that the Russians take as much as possible of their quota in Norwegian waters where the Norwegian Coast Guard enforces fisheries regulations.
52.   *NordNews.ru*, 10 September 2010 (accessed 5 February 2012).
53.   *Vzgljad*, 27 April 2010.
54.   *Murmanskij vestnik*, 7 May 2010.
55.   *NordNews.ru*, 18 October 2010 (accessed 5 February 2012).
56.   *NordNews*, 23 November 2010.
57.   *Murmanskij vestnik*, 18 November 2010.

6. Discussion: two levels of discourses in Russian environmental policy

MAJOR DISCOURSES

Climate Change

We have defined four major discourses in the Russian debate on climate change, related to *benefits, threats, rationality* and *fairness*.

Interestingly, the possible benefits for Russia seem to be taken as a point of departure for the participants in the debate, whether they are for or against Russian participation in the international collaboration under the Kyoto Protocol or its flexible mechanisms. These benefits may relate to direct investment, a positive image for Russia in the international community, or compensation for the 'ecological services' provided by Russia's forests.

The potential threats to Russia, on the other hand, are cited by proponents and opponents of Russia in the international climate regime, each seeking to prove the other side wrong. Opponents claim that Russian participation would imply limitations on emission growth that could hamper economic development in the country, making it difficult, for instance, to reach the goal of doubling the gross domestic product (GDP). Supporters of the Kyoto Protocol see this as unrealistic in any event and argue that non-participation would involve loss of competitiveness in the global market. Opponents also suspect Western motives behind the climate regime, suggesting Western governments are ultimately aiming to make Russia dependent on their technologies, or seeking access to Russia's natural resources. In short, the threats are perceived as economic and political rather than environmental.

Further, the Russian debate is characterized by significant climate scepticism: indeed the rationality of the entire regime is questioned. Contrary to Western interpretations of this scepticism, however, the Russian argument refers not so much to the scientific assumption that climate change is human-induced, but to the inability of the regime to generate sufficient emissions reductions to stop climate change, due to the limited global coverage of the Kyoto Protocol. All the same, Russian scientists promote a more holistic approach to climate change than the Intergovernmental Panel on Climate Change (IPCC), keeping the options open to alternative explanations. The possible positive effects of climate change also figure more prominently in the public debate in Russia than in the West. Thus, the Russian approach includes analysis of different explanations of climate change and of both positive and negative consequences, and is considered by Russians to be more balanced than Western approaches.

Related to the rationality discourse, the fairness of the international climate partnership is questioned. Although Russia formally recognizes the principle of 'common but differentiated responsibilities', it does not accept that emerging economies of the G77 developing country group should be exempt from obligations.

Protecting the Baltic Sea Environment

In the Russian debate on the international collaboration to protect the Baltic Sea environment, we summarized the prevailing storylines into more general discourse on benefits, Russia's great power status, the fairness of the collaboration and its environmental effects. An underlying premise in the debate is that Russia should benefit from the international partnership in some way or another; the Baltic Sea regime has throughout its history been valued primarily in terms of its political and economic gains. In the initial phase, for instance, the Soviets pressed for Western recognition of the German Democratic Republic – an objective far beyond the realm of environmental protection. In the 1990s, the Russians called for Western investments – including direct subsidies, technical support and international loans – as preconditions for further cooperation. While some participants in the debate emphasize the win-win character of the international regime, others see Russia as taking advantage of 'silly Western concerns' for the Baltic Sea environment. Industry effects on the environment are usually framed as *health* issues in Russia: and the consequences for human health of environmental degradation in the Baltic Sea have been negligible, at least for Russia. In the internal Russian debate, non-governmental organizations (NGOs) have criticized their own authorities for seeking only financial benefits from the international cooperation, and for using an environmental forum for other purposes, like advancing Russian energy exports.

A similarly recurring theme over the years has been Russia's role as a great power. Geopolitical concerns were particularly strong in the early years of cooperation, but re-emerged after the enlargement of the EU in 2004. The Helsinki Commission (HELCOM), and Baltic Sea cooperation more widely (in the Council of the Baltic Sea States (CBSS)), were now seen as a buffer against the rising EU influence in the region. These

geopolitical motivations have been openly articulated, and cooperation is seen as a game in which the balance of power is the main logic of
operation. Russia's perception of itself as a great power is reflected in its
attempts to deny obvious environmental degradation and focus instead
on its positive contributions to the Baltic Sea environment: its biodiversity
and established nature reserves. More importantly perhaps, the Russian
authorities have accused NGO collaboration with Western partners of
espionage, underlining the need for Russians to stand together in order to
maintain the country's global image. Labelling Russia an environmental
laggard obviously works against this. Also, Russia has been reluctant to
take upon itself obligations that it might not be able to meet, as that could
harm its image abroad.

The partnership discourse revolves around the equality of status among
the collaborating partners. Again, labelling Russia as an environmental
laggard is opposed and the country's achievements in environmental protection are underscored. Unlike the great power discourse, the aim here
is not to demonstrate Russia's superiority compared to other nations,
but simply to protect its status as an equal partner in the regime. The
process of cooperation is seen as a goal of its own, contributing to building confidence among the participating countries. And unlike the benefits
discourse, Russian independence is emphasized and Western *Besserwissers*
are despised. Small-scale projects, informal meetings and day-to-day
contact are appreciated. The cooperation in fact empowers Russia to take
its own share of the costs of environmental protection.

Strictly environmental concerns are also voiced in the debate, and some
actors point out that environmental protection is in fact the ultimate
objective of the international cooperation. Russia is unable to protect the
Baltic Sea environment on its own: outside help is necessary. As in the
benefits discourse, however, some environmental challenges are framed
differently in Russia than in the West. In particular, certain challenges are
seen as 'first-class' problems precisely because they attract the attention of
the West – the Russian domestic impact is downplayed. As a consequence,
many problems that affect people in their everyday lives are not given
sufficient priority as seen from a strictly environmental perspective. The
environmental challenge is accepted, but other concerns dictate action.
That said, scientific evidence is generally seen as the main justification for
political action within this discourse.

Fisheries Management in the Barents Sea

Fisheries management differs from climate-change mitigation and environmental protection since it, by definition, involves sharing of benefits

rather than distribution of burdens (except in situations where fish stocks have been decimated). As regards the Barents Sea regime, managed bilaterally by Norway and Russia and generally seen as one of the most effective international fisheries management regimes globally, we have noted two main discourses, both centring on sharing of benefits among parties. More than the biological viability of fish stocks and petty regulatory measures, however, they reflect concern with Russia's place in the world and the rules of the game in international politics. We have distinguished between a malign and a benign variant of a 'zero-sum game' discourse. The underlying premise is that states are constantly involved in the pursuit of political and economic goods, and that one state's gain will always involve a loss for other states. While the cooperation atmosphere has generally been good between Norway and Russia as regards management of the Barents Sea fish stocks, in the Russian debate Norway has been presented as the cunning neighbour who talks in politically correct terms of sustainability and precaution, but ultimately aims at boosting its own profit at the expense of the Russian fishing industry. In the malign variant of the zero-sum game discourse, Norway is portrayed as a Western country engaged in a Cold War-like (or 'Cold Peace') battle against Russia, preoccupied above all with ruining the Russian economy; even if Norway sees its own profit reduced, it is the winner of the game as long as Russia loses more. Here Norway is seen as a NATO country primarily promoting the interests of the West, with the sustainability of fish stocks as a secondary motive. In the more benign variant, the security aspect is downplayed, and Norway is seen more as a fair-playing good neighbour: a rational state that does not necessarily have any evil intentions but simply takes advantage of the international rules of the game to protect its own interests. In both the malign and the benign version, interestingly enough, Norway is established as an ideal for Russia: this is simply how states are expected to behave in international politics.

Participants in the debate also underline the fundamentally good relations between the two northern neighbours. The two countries 'breathe in sync', according to some observers. And, at least in scientific circles, there is no major disagreement between the parties, and little (if any) suspicion of hidden motives. Rather than sharp divisions, there is a sliding passage between the three discourses: from the malign to the benign variant of zero-sum thinking, and further to the joint benefit discourse. In all three, the potential for mutual gain is reflected, although at the more 'malign' end of the continuum, win-win situations are presented as rare, at least in difficult times when fish stocks are threatened. The joint benefit discourse places good neighbourly relations in the foreground, but the fact that Norway belongs to a different strategic alliance is still a factor to be reckoned with, and Russians need to keep a close eye on their Western neighbours.

Overarching Discourses

'Benefits', 'pride' and 'science' are key words in the Russian discourses on climate change, marine environmental protection and fisheries management. Russian benefits – 'what's in it for us' – seem central in all three issue areas. In the climate and marine environmental protection discourses, this is the underlying premise of the debate; in the fisheries case, it is the point of departure for the regime as such. Inherent in these discourses is the assumption that international environmental regimes are arenas where Russia can, and should, promote its more general interests, economically and politically. On occasion, the Soviet Union/Russian Federation has pressed for political solutions entirely outside the scope of the regimes in question. More often, economic benefit is sought from the West in the form of subsidies, loans and investments. Such concessions are fully expected and deemed perfectly justified in return for supporting an international environmental regime that is understood to be in the interest of the other participants rather than of Russia. In only one of our cases have Russian NGOs opposed this approach.

'Pride' figures in several variants in the debates; it is partly linked to the benefits discourse and relates to both political and economic interests. However, the focus is not primarily (at least not explicitly) on financial gain, but on Russia's prestige in the global community, in particular its role as great power – or at least its status as an equal partner with Western governments. In the Baltic Sea regimes, Russia has used the specific international institutional platforms to offset EU influence in the region. The fact that this has been openly articulated underscores the extent to which it is seen as a 'natural thing' in Russia to speak of environmental regimes as primarily arenas for wider political ambitions. As we observed in the fisheries case, the debate has centred more (at least implicitly) on Russia's place in the world and the rules of the game in international politics, than on biology and regulation. The question is not so much what's in it for Russia in terms of money, but how national pride can best be defended. Inherent here is the assumption that the outside world is forever trying to take advantage of Russia, often under the guise of environmental protection and other politically correct terms. Sometimes 'they' are after Russia's natural resources; sometimes 'they' aim to reduce Russia's market share in the global community or make Russia economically dependent on the West; and sometimes 'they' simply want to inflict harm on the Russian economy or Russia's political clout and image internationally, because – according to this line of thinking – it is always in one state's interest if other states are made to see their standing lowered. It is assumed that Western governments use 'soft' actors such as environmental NGOs for espionage in their quest for power and for reducing Russia's reputation in the international community. Likewise, it is claimed that Western governments exaggerate environmental degradation in Russia while downplaying their own problems, in order to blacken Russia's reputation. These Western actions can harm the Russian economy, but more than anything they serve to humiliate Russia in the eyes of the global community.

Russia and the West are interchangeably seen as 'silly', in both the (related) benefits and power discourses: Russia takes advantage of what it perceives as the stupid and scientifically unfounded Western concern about the environment to request financial assistance (Baltic Sea), while Western shrewdness in some cases comes at the expense of Russian naïveté (Barents Sea).

Ideally, scientific knowledge should be the main foundation for political action in environmental protection, at least from a biological point of view. In our fisheries case, the scientific recommendations from the International Council for the Exploration of the Sea underlie the setting of quotas for the Barents Sea stocks. These recommendations are generally, although not always, used by the Joint Norwegian-Russian Fisheries Commission in its quota setting. Relations between Norwegian and Russian scientists are reported to be good – but, interestingly enough, the tight integration of Russia's northwestern regional fisheries research institute in the global scientific community has been seen as suspicious and has been challenged by the federal Russian fisheries research institute. Again, we see how science, economy and national prestige are intertwined. In the climate case, Russian scientists do not challenge the global consensus on anthropogenic climate change, but they do call for a more holistic approach. By and large, science has been incorporated in the international regimes; Russian and Western scientific approaches do not differ significantly; and the major discursive battles are not in the 'softer' scientific field, but in the 'harder' fields of economic benefit and political prestige.

In sum, we can observe three main discursive clusters that are not sharply divided but follow along a continuum. The role of science is always present in the discourse – but so are economic benefits and national pride. At one end of the spectrum, international environmental regimes are seen as arenas for ongoing battles between Russia and the West about money and prestige, with science as a foil for interest-based decisions. At the other end, science is taken as the point of departure for political action, while the actual outcomes are coloured by economic and political interests. In the cases examined here, discursive concentration is found at the former end of the continuum. International environmental regimes are explicitly referred to as natural arenas for money games; implicitly, the defence of national pride is omnipresent; and science figures as a not completely irrelevant factor in policy-making.

COMPARISON OF THE CASE REGIMES

Despite the common elements found in the cases and the overarching discourses introduced above, we also find differences between the cases that are crucial for understanding the dynamics of Russia's performance in international environmental politics. We have approached the question of whether Russia's actions in the international arenas of environmental policy are motivated by environmental or other interests through case studies of three very different regimes: fisheries, the Baltic Sea protection, and climate change. The dynamics and frameworks under which these regimes operate are an important starting point for our discussion as they have implications for case comparability – whether Russia's actions under the regimes are motivated by similar or different circumstances. This section evaluates the differences in terms of coverage, rationale, types of burdens, their rigidity, domestic consequences of Russia's commitments, and the role of science in the Russian debate.

The obvious difference between the regimes is their *coverage*. The fact that the fishing regime is a bilateral one between Russia and Norway limits the number of parties and requires active participation on the part of Russia. It also makes the burdens and benefits – and their fairness – very transparent to the participants. This becomes blurred already in the case of the regional Baltic Sea protection regime. However, the EU as Russia's counterpart also introduces geopolitical interests related to the regime, serving to promote active participation. The global approach of the climate regime makes Russia just one more industrialized country participant (albeit significant as the fourth largest emitter in the world) and enables Russia to adopt a more marginal role, waiting to see the positions taken by others before deciding on its own approach. However, Russia's decisive role in bringing the Kyoto Protocol into force broke this routine. Also, given the large number of participants, the source of benefits – who ends up paying – is less obvious, as are the national implications of the burdens adopted. Thus, under global regimes it is easier to disregard the efforts of others than under regimes with fewer participants.

The *rationale of the regime* varies, although the environment is an important factor in all three. For the fisheries regime, the primary task is to define the total quota of fish available in a sustainable manner without jeopardizing future stocks, and to divide this economic benefit between the two countries. Understandings of what is 'sustainable' have differed between the parties. The starting point for the Baltic Sea regime is indeed environmentally motivated: protection of the Baltic Sea environment. However, when the regime was originally set up, geopolitical interests provided an additional motivation. It was difficult to create a good discussion platform between the Soviet Union and the West, and environmental cooperation was considered as a 'soft' non-politicized topic that could facilitate space for discussions on other, more political, topics as well. And third, the climate regime has been established because of environmental concerns as to the dangerous impacts of climate change, with the aim defined as reducing the cause of the problem, greenhouse gas emissions, in a globally fair manner. This task requires both defining a cap to global emissions and sharing burdens between parties. Here the environmental rationale converts into economics: a division of the rights to welfare and development between the parties.

By *the types of burdens* we refer to the degree of bindingness of the regimes. The type of burden, due to its economic and political consequences in the case of non-compliance, is an important element in considering participation in a regime. Under the Baltic regime, the Helsinki Convention and the Baltic Sea Action Plan are binding as such, but recommendations – the real instrument guiding activities – make implementation voluntary; there are no sanctions against non-compliance. Under the fisheries regime, commitments are monitored by the two parties; if one party does not comply (which would basically mean pulling out of the regime), that will not necessarily have economic implications in the short run, because both parties could then fish as much as they please. Complying with commitments is enforced by sanctions under the climate regime and lead to economic consequences under the regime. Having said this, it should be noted that the actual ability of international regimes to enforce their obligations, even when these are seen as internationally legally binding, is questionable when the parties in question are sovereign countries.

Also the *rigidity of commitments* is highly relevant here: does compliance actually require costly implementation of domestic measures? Under the fishing regime, it is necessary to limit the economic activities of domestic stakeholders in order to achieve the agreed quotas. In the case of the Baltic Sea protection regime, most of the measures implemented by Russia so far have not required much extra effort; also the existing requirements set by the Baltic Sea Action Plan for Russia have generally been met by modernizing sewage treatment facilities – which would probably have be done in any case, with or without the regime. As the climate regime takes 1990 as the year of comparison – one year after the Soviet Union collapsed, together with many of its polluting activities – Russia's commitment to not exceed this level by 2012 was very easy and implied no direct costs to ensure compliance. By contrast, Russia's pledge for 2020 – to limit emissions to 15–25 per cent below the 1990 level – would have required some domestic measures. That Moscow rejected the second phase of the Kyoto Protocol indicates that, among other things, complying with the target was seen as too uncertain, or at least unfairly demanding in comparison to other countries.

Comparison of the *domestic consequences of Russia's commitments* provides further understanding of the impact of the various regimes from Russian stakeholders' point of view. The expectation of the nature of the consequences – burden, benefit or none at all – is a relevant factor in terms of motivation for participating. Further, perceived opportunities for influencing domestic political decisions are also linked to the unity of the target groups. The fishing quotas mostly influence a small, focused and quite local branch of industry, and are perceived as a limitation on economic activity. The stakeholders here are directly aware of the consequences of the quotas set, and have been motivated and able to organize themselves as a lobby. In the case of the climate regime, Russia's easy initial target put no burden on any domestic stakeholders; however, the benefits available motivated them to attempt influencing in the domestic policy-making process. The more focused group of project developers made attempts to influence political decisions concerning the Kyoto regime, while the dispersed group of industrial companies was less vocal, or became involved mostly as a result of the initiative by the project developer group. The Baltic Sea regime commitments have not generated a group of Russian stakeholders directly influenced economically, given the financial support of EU countries to Russian compliance. The beneficiaries of these financial streams were not organized and did not try to influence domestic political decision-making, perhaps due to their primary links to the regional and local administrations rather than to the federal government.

The *role of science*, or how it is understood in the Russian discussion, also varies significantly in the three regimes. The scientific understanding of environmental problems of the Baltic Sea, such as eutrophication, is considered as solid by all parties, which has provided an easy starting point for the Baltic Sea protection regime. However, it should be noted that, because the cooperation brings financial benefits, it would probably have been accepted by Russia even if there were disagreement on science. The outcome of the fisheries regime is closely linked to scientific consensus between the parties. A spell of scientific disagreement between the parties led to short-term differences in the interpretation of the maximum sustainable fishing quota and Russia rejecting the internationally accepted approach to quota setting in favour of a less precautionary interpretation by some domestic scientists. Under the climate regime, the Russian stakeholders have basically agreed to question the rigidity of the Western precautionary approach to science. However, as the Kyoto first commitment period provided benefits to Russia, the issue of burden-sharing did not limit its participation, and the scientific debate could be viewed as quite detached from Russia's position under the regime. Table 6.1 summarizes the comparison between the regimes.

In sum, Russia has most to lose under the fisheries regime in the short term and under the climate regime in the long term. The benefits beyond burden-sharing are most evident in the climate and Baltic Sea protection regimes, whereas domestic stakeholders are directly influenced by the burdens accepted under the fisheries regime only. This is also the sole commitment what can be considered as environmentally rigid. The climate and Baltic Sea regimes have given Russia an easy ride in terms of commitments – some foreign observers have even seen Russia's commitment under the Kyoto Protocol as a free ride. The climate and Baltic Sea regimes have provided opportunities for interested domestic stakeholders, best organized in the fishery and climate cases due to the economic consequences that followed the regimes. Also in these cases, science has caused most disagreement while entailing practical consequences for only the fisheries regime.

TWO-LEVEL GAME

Is There a Two-Level Game?

From what we have learned from the case studies about the interplay between the domestic and executive levels as regards policy formation, it seems obvious that Putnam's original two-level game idea (see Chapter 2) of the executive trying to accommodate both domestic and international interests has not been reality when it comes to Russia and the cases examined here. Domestic debates have seemed quite detached from executive-level decisions – as follows naturally from the non-democratic nature of the Russian political system. However, this does not necessarily mean that Putnam's original way of thinking is totally inapplicable to the case of Russia. It can offer a useful starting point for discussion.

To evaluate whether domestic debate influences policy decisions, we must see whether the case studies offer any evidence of domestic pressure on the executive, as outlined by the concept of two-level game. Such

Table 6.1 Comparison between regimes

	Coverage	Rationale	Type/rigidity of burdens	Domestic consequences of Russia's commitments	Role of science in Russian debate
Fisheries	Bilateral	To define the annual sustainable fishing quota and divide it between Russia and Norway	Binding: non-compliance at state level would entail pulling out of the regime, nullifying it	Economic burden to small, focused industry	Dispute between Russian scientific institutes on sustainability, attached to defining quotas
Baltic Sea	Regional	To reduce eutrophication in the Baltic Sea and create a platform for 'soft' foreign-policy cooperation	Convention binding in itself, but its recommendations are mainly voluntary	Economic benefits to dispersed beneficiaries/ economic burdens dispersed and minor as supported by Western subsidies	Consensus on science, detached from benefits
Climate change	Global	To avoid dangerous environmental impacts of climate change in a fair manner	Binding for industrialized country group (Annex I) participants/no implementation required	Economic benefits to focused and dispersed beneficiaries, economic burden possible in the future	Scepticism to Western approach to science, detached from benefits

Source: Authors.

pressure can be verified if it can be shown that policy was formed as a result of it. In our case studies, only one clear example emerges. With the fisheries case, the coalition formed by the local fishery industry and the sceptical wing of domestic scientists was allowed to control Russia's negotiations of fishing quotas with Norway. However, after the turn of the millennium, the central Moscow machinery took over again, shifting the policy back to favour the internationally approved scientific norms. Here the incentive may have come from the rising geopolitical interest in Arctic cooperation with Norway, referring to the delimitation agreement adopted in 2010.

That said, most of our findings go in the opposite direction.

In the climate case, lively domestic debate – in what seemed to be a bargaining process – took place, especially with regard to ratification of the Kyoto Protocol, and further, on whether Russia should join the second phase of the Protocol. And yet, the apparently dominant domestic discourses lost the battle both times: premised on EU support to Russian World Trade Organization (WTO) membership and more general image benefits, the Kyoto Protocol was ratified against the advice of Russian scientists as well as the lobby, underlining the lack of participation by others. Although the ongoing economic benefits from continuing joint implementation (JI) projects would have favoured joining Kyoto II, the pact was rejected on the grounds of its low coverage, that is the absence of other key players. Also here, more ambitious commitment may have played a role.

Domestic debate about the Barents Sea fisheries has been extensive in Russia, focusing mainly on the need for higher quotas to combat the 'exaggerated' precaution favoured by Norway. Except for a short period around the turn of the millennium, the proponents of raising quotas above scientifically recommended levels have not been able to define the Russian negotiation position. Moreover, the substantial criticism from fisheries circles concerning the 2010 Barents Sea delimitation agreement with Norway has had no effect on national policy.

Finally, executive interests in foreign policy were what initiated the Baltic Sea cooperation. As the regime put little economic pressure on any domestic actor groups, it gave rise to little domestic debate or attempts to influence policy-making. However, Moscow may have considered the profile of HELCOM sufficiently positive, since it was seen as a suitable forum for pushing for Russian geopolitical interests – as in energy transport, when lobbying for the Nordstream pipeline.

Thus we may say the foreign policy and geopolitical interests of the executive level (including the objective of demonstrating that Russia is a responsible player in international politics) drive policy and position formation in Russia, rather than pressures from lower-level domestic stakeholders. The economic interests of domestic actor groups are secondary; however, if a regime is not linked to such interests, then lower-level economic benefits may drive decision-making, as shown by the fisheries case study on at least one occasion and the Baltic Sea case throughout the 1990s. In the decisions themselves, environmental arguments do not appear as drivers (for further analysis, see Chapter 7); this would indicate that they rank below domestic economic interests.

Returning to Putnam's theoretical proposition of a two-level game, we agree with Henry and McIntosh Sundstrom (2012, p. 1317) that there is not much domestic bargaining involved in formulating Russia's foreign environmental policy. Further, they argue that in Russia, the relevant actors of international environmental politics are limited to the federal level, ultimately to the leadership. The relevance of private economic actors tends to be very limited, let alone that of environmental NGOs. It could even be argued that the detached domestic level is some kind of third, less relevant, level in the game. If a regime ends up being considered as irrelevant from a foreign policy perspective, domestic interests may gain power. Also when the executive level takes decisions on the basis of foreign policy interests, some other argumentations can be picked from the domestic debate. This opportunity supports participation in the debate, regardless of its low level of importance.

The 'flow' of pressure can be seen as absent in the direction from the domestic debate towards the executive, whereas the other 'flows' of pressure – from the executive towards domestic actors and international actors, and from international actors towards the executive – basically apply as outlined by Putnam. Thus, the main adjustment to Putnam's two-level game that seems required is to treat the domestic level game as some kind of 'bad phone connection'. Sometimes arguments from that level are heard, sometimes not: moreover, the choice of the executive between these argumentations is random, rather than based on success in domestic-level bargaining, which we observed as dominating discourses.

However, this has not always been the case in Russia. As a result of the presidential determination to strengthen the vertical of power since the turn of the millennium, high-ranking civil servants have now at least partly superseded local actors. The Baltic Sea and the fisheries cases, dating back to the 1990s and the 1970s respectively, strongly reflect the changing patterns of the power of influence of domestic actors. In both cases, regional and local actors were influential in defining Russia's position in the regimes during the 1990s when a general decentralization trend prevailed, with more power given to the regions. In the Baltic Sea case, this implied an autonomous role for the St Petersburg water and sewage utility, which established contacts with foreign partners independent of the authorities – the federal ones were not interested, and the local and regional ones lacked financial and human resources to control interaction. In the fisheries case, the lobby of regional actors was allowed to form Russia's position for a short period.

Approaching the Russian decision-making system from the two-level game angle, we divide the further discussion into domestic and international policy levels. Here it must be kept in mind that stakeholders on these levels tend to be quite detached from each other, and that the lower level is just as much an audience to executive-level rhetoric as are foreign actors.

Discourses *vis-à-vis* Domestic Policy Level

The three cases analysed in this book differ from each other significantly with regard to the amount of domestic policy bargaining. In the Baltic Sea case, there was almost no domestic bargaining; in the fishery case, we noted fisheries industry interest groups in the regions trying to advance their business interests, versus the federal administration in Moscow with its focus on the geopolitical, and not least, diplomatic aspects. In the case of climate policy, considerable domestic policy bargaining seems to have taken place among various actors; however, the dominant bargaining points were chosen by the top leadership mainly in order to support their own geopolitically driven decisions.

Despite the moderate amount of policy bargaining, in each of our cases the strongly evolving benefits discourse relates to domestic policy-making and is used primarily to appeal to the domestic audience and justify Russian participation in the international regime at hand. In particular, this is so when benefits are framed in terms of economic gains. In the Baltic Sea case, energy transport via the Baltic Sea as well as foreign investments in wastewater treatment and modernization of other infrastructure have been heavily underlined as part of the benefits discourse. This links directly in with the overall modernization campaign of the Russian leadership. The same applies to the climate case, where the expected revenues from the carbon market as well as energy-efficiency improvements were framed as a path towards technological modernization and cost savings, rather than as dealing with actual environmental policy. In the first decade of the 2000s, it was generally acknowledged that adducing climate-related arguments in domestic bargaining could reduce the chances that a policy or an initiative would be accepted: such interests were mostly phrased as 'modernization' initiatives.

Further, the benefits achieved have chiefly been non-environmental. In the fisheries case, the entire rationale for regime is to divide economic benefits (fishing quotas); the environmental angle enters when discussing the method of determining these quotas. In the climate case, the discourse is driven mainly by the benefits that can accrue to Russia from the regime; the general assumption in Russia has been that the whole Kyoto pact is simply about economics, for all participants. This even led the Russian debate to raise the issue of getting 'guarantees' of benefits that have been 'promised' to Russia under the regime – an idea totally alien to other Kyoto participants. A major difference was that, unlike the Baltic Sea protection case, nobody in Russia questioned the benefits-based starting point of the discussion. The environmental discourse criticized the lack of domestic environmental concern and focus on maximizing benefits from environmental projects.

We find a striking lack of discourses that centre on environmental concerns. The only case in which a specific environment discourse can actually be discerned is that of the Baltic Sea cooperation. The reason may well be the low priority of the issue to the highest Russian leadership: because Baltic Sea environmental concerns are of low importance, also the general public and NGOs can take part in the discussions – not directly in defining Russia's position within the regime, but in the media at least. Also the character of the environmental problem in question matters: a polluted sea is much easier for human senses to comprehend and experience than a changing climate or the size of fish stocks. Further evidence is also provided by the Russian focus on specific local wastewater issues rather than the more abstract concept of eutrophication, which is the main focus of the Baltic Sea regime. Also, it is often argued in Russia that scientific facts on the environmental problem and its impacts must be presented in order to justify domestic policy action. This condition was fulfilled by the Baltic Sea regime, and fisheries regime after a domestic struggle. On the issue of climate change, however, it has not been fulfilled.

The fact that the dominant discourses relate primarily to economic policy goals at the domestic level indicates that low priority is accorded to environmental issues in the Russian political hierarchy, on the one hand, and the low level of participation of actors beyond the authorities and business actors, on the other. Also the low interest on the part of the general public in environmental, especially global level, problems supports this. Further, it also suggests that Russia's engagement in international environmental politics is motivated by other than environmental concerns. The discourses that underscore the threats that the regime in question may pose often relate to a domestic policy goal as well. For example in the climate case, opponents fear that restrictions set by the Kyoto regime could obstruct Russian economic development (for example, the goal of doubling the GDP), and lead to a loss of competitiveness in the global market. By contrast, Kyoto proponents see the restrictions as a means of achieving economic effectiveness, and (although this is not spelled out very clearly by the actors themselves) private profit from JI project implementation. Here we see the very same domestic policy goal used to argue for opposing lines of action, although the private interests motivating the arguments differ.

Discourses *vis-à-vis* the Foreign Policy Level

The discourses drawing on national pride, in turn, relate primarily to Russia's foreign policy motives and the dynamics of negotiation within the regimes in question. The vitality of these 'pride' discourses shows that geopolitics is an important part of Russia's performance in international environmental politics, regardless of the environmental problem at hand. This is well in line with Putin's foreign policy vision (see Chapter 2), where preservation of the global balance of power and national sovereignty are important foreign policy goals, as well as control of the use of soft power – the attractiveness of the country's international image.

'Pride' discourses appear strongest in the fisheries case: here the dominant discourses reflect concern over Russia's role in the world and the rules of the game in international politics (zero-sum game). The strong prevalence of this discourse may be related to the fact that the fisheries regime is about the governance of a natural resource; natural resources are traditionally understood as the basic geopolitical factors. Also the two other cases reflect Russia's concern over its place and role in the world, relating to more general foreign policy goals and paradigms of thought. In the climate case, global fairness arises as a major discourse, mainly in justifying Russian non-participation based on the non-participation of others. Also in the Baltic Sea case, where cooperation has proceeded smoothly, the pride discourse is evident in the form of the great power discourse – especially after the latest EU enlargement. All other countries in the Baltic region are now EU members, and Russia is against such 'EU dominance'; thus, it supports HELCOM as a means of power balancing in the region.

National pride and great power balancing are underlined also by downplaying Western environmental motives and underlining that Russians are no 'worse' than Western actors; Russians are keen to demonstrate that also the latter have self-interest driven motives for their performance within the regimes. This includes the idea that Western actors have 'hidden real intentions' and may use environmental concern as a smokescreen to achieve other goals. Norway's perceived desire to 'destroy' Russia was considered by some Russians to be hidden behind the environmental concern in the fisheries case, and the Kyoto scheme was seen as a plot to control Russia and its economic growth. It appeared extremely hard for some Russian stakeholders to believe that in other countries (especially in the EU) climate policies can be incentivized by genuine environmental concern, and Kyoto was labelled as 'economic rather than environmental agreement' in the Russian debate. Underlying this attitude seems to have been a belief in Russia's own approach of using environmental arguments largely as tools for image-building or justifying actions that are, in reality, motivated by other interests.

In some cases, Russia's greatness is held to be based on its ecological superiority, and Russian discourses often consider and see it as unfair that Westerners hold Russia to be an environmental laggard. Compliance with its international level commitments tends to be a matter of pride for Russia, which is manifested loudly – even regardless of the rigidity of target. Under the Kyoto Protocol, Russia's performance was widely seen as flawed, due to its unrealistically easy target defined by the final days of the Soviet Union – a view rejected by Moscow, which emphasized that Russia's emission collapse was the most significant contribution to emissions reductions in global terms that have been made. The same approach, protecting the reputation of a great power, also works even when Russia's laggardness is obvious. For instance, in the Baltic Sea case, nutrient leakages identified by foreigners were ignored or denied. Russian actors are also keen to cite examples of Western laggardness or non-performance. Russia's above-mentioned emissions decline was considered as the top performance at the global level; here it was pointed out that some major emitters (the US, China) were not participating at all. Thus, the Kyoto Protocol was considered as 'discriminatory' against Russia, a point held to justify Russian withdrawal from the second phase.

On the other hand, and quite the opposite of geopolitically-biased thinking, Russia has not hesitated to take advantage of its 'laggardness'; as in the Baltic Sea case, where support and grants were welcome to modernize sewage treatment, which is considered one of the basic services of 'civilized' societies. In the fisheries case, the Russians leaned on their weak economic position to get acceptance for higher quotas; in the climate case, Russia has considered the gains stemming from its economic collapse that followed the end of the Soviet Union as a legitimate environmental contribution that justifies expecting benefits from the Kyoto regime. Nor are environmental arguments that are expected – or known – to be central to the Western actors often used as a supportive argument to other political goals (as in the case of the Nord Stream gas pipeline).

While this approach stands in stark contrast to the foreign-policy approach emphasizing Russia's greatness and national pride, it is well in line with the pro-Western liberal approach to foreign policy, pragmatism in particular (see Chapter 2). The pragmatic foreign-policy approach underscores partnerships and confidence-building through bottom-up efforts like scientific cooperation. This pragmatic approach is stronger in the fisheries and Baltic Sea cases than in the climate case – which is natural, as the level of cooperation in the former two cases is bilateral or regional (neighbourhood, with emphasis on such issues), whereas the climate issue is seen more as a zero-sum battle over benefits between various countries participating in the international treaty. On the other hand, the JI mechanism did provide such a pragmatic field for cooperation on climate.

Dynamics Between the Two Levels

Vladimir Putin's foreign policy vision sees Russia's foreign policy as a derived function of domestic policy: the major aim is to advance the internal development of the country. Our scrutiny of the three cases and how they are reflected in domestic and foreign policy levels has shown that domestic and foreign policies are interlinked also in Russia's engagement in international environmental politics. While the pride discourse is linked to the foreign-policy approach that emphasizes Russia's greatness and national image (soft power), it is also at the core of domestic politics: the leadership is eager to demonstrate the country's great power status, primarily to Russia's own people. Also the aim of achieving economic benefits and overall modernization is related to the aspirations of domestic as well as foreign policy: as Russia becomes more prosperous, it will also be more respected abroad – and with greater influence in international politics.

By contrast, the influence of international environmental politics and discourses on Russia's domestic environmental policy and discourses on the problems appears minimal, at least in the cases examined in this book. As noted also by Mol (2009, p. 237), Russian leaders seem quite capable of resisting environmental demands coming from abroad.

Science discourse provides a good example of the interplay between the domestic and foreign policy levels. Our case studies have shown how Russian and Western scientific approaches actually do not differ significantly – but scientific arguments are used differently at the domestic level and international level, depending on the discussion in question. Scientific environmental knowledge as such does not offer a firm foundation for political action in Russia: it is intertwined with discourses on benefits and pride, underscoring the absence of purely environmental motivations in the instances examined here.

In both the climate and the fisheries cases, Russians have at times questioned Western science, thereby supplementing the pride discourse with ideas of Russian superiority in the field of science as well.

It is true, in the fishery case, that the majority of influential scientists came out in favour of the precautionary principle, but that is not to say that there was Russian environmental concern behind this approval. No, the important elements for Russia's approval were the economic benefits from fishing and the geopolitical benefits of reaching a compromise with Norway. However, Russians also tend to see environmental issues as scientific-technical rather than socio-political; and we find Russian acceptance in the instances where there is no politics involved but decisions are based on 'pure scientific facts'.

In the climate case, the entire regime was questioned, on the basis of the scientific argument that the regime's efforts were insufficient to slow down climate change. However, Russian actors may well have voiced this argument so enthusiastically in order to add to Russia's bargaining power at the international level. With evidence showing that the Kyoto regime was not going to solve the environmental problem, it became more legitimate to require compensation in return for bringing it into force. Here the assumption was again that the policies driving the main proponents of the Kyoto Protocol were based on concerns other than purely environmental ones.

7. Conclusion: environmental encounters?

Are Russia's encounters with international environmental agreements not purely environmental, but reflect more general foreign and domestic policy goals, and sometimes used as 'platforms' for image-building and benefit-seeking rather promoting environmental goals? That was the question underlying the major hypothesis posed in the beginning of this book. We have indeed found evidence to support our hypothesis in all three cases presented here: the Kyoto climate regime, the Baltic Sea cooperation, and the Joint Norwegian-Russian Fisheries Commission.

With the climate case, the evidence indicates that Russia's motivations for joining the Kyoto Protocol were related to the country's international image and its desire to be admitted to the World Trade Organization (WTO), rather than trying to solve the problem and avoid the impacts of climate change. Similarly, participation in the Kyoto joint implementation (JI) was driven by the economic interests of domestic businesses and administration. In terms of the ultimate drivers of Russia's policy, the foreign policy benefits appear to have been decisive, whereas the economic benefits were considered as merely an additional dividend. Russia ratified the Kyoto Protocol, enabling it to take effect, but then rejected its second phase – even though the same economic benefits would have been more certain under Kyoto II. Environmental argumentation in terms of concern about the anticipated environmental impacts was almost completely absent in the domestic discourses. However, the total impact of the climate regime in terms of halting climate change was brought in as a counter-argument based on ecological rationality: it was claimed that regime coverage would be insufficient to influence concentrations of greenhouse gases in the atmosphere. Also, environmental arguments were used to obtain benefits from foreign actors, as through the JI project mechanism, and at the international level to underline Russia's leading role as a 'green' contributor to global politics by bringing the Kyoto Protocol into force.

With the joint Norwegian-Russian commission for managing the Barents Sea fisheries, the inherent driver has been to regulate fisheries sustainably, so that they will continue to represent an economic good in the future. Environmental concerns – the willingness to manage fish stocks sustainably – have been reflected in the Russian debate about the management of the Barents Sea fish stocks, though mostly implicitly. Both parties to the regime have taken the task of sustainable fisheries management seriously: they base the quota setting on scientific advice, and have generally followed the recommendations from Norwegian and Russian scientific institutes, coordinated between the two parties and peer-reviewed at the international level in the International Council for the Exploration of the Sea (ICES). But the Russian discourse on the Barents Sea fisheries is very much about more general relations with the West (here, Norway), and it cannot be said that Russian policies have been motivated by environmental concern. Almost without exception, the Russia media debate has focused on Norway's intentions in the collaborative regime, and Russia's standing in the international community. Science, including the objective of sustainability, is also debated from this perspective: to what extent it supports Russian interests in the game of international politics.

Also in the case of Baltic Sea cooperation, our analysis indicates that Russia's motivations for participating stem mainly from the economic and image benefits. The main drivers of policy have evolved over time: in the 1970s and 1980s, foreign policy benefits were at the forefront; during the 1990s, economic benefits, such as foreign investment in the urban water infrastructure, were of particular importance. More recently, economic benefits, especially those related to energy exports, have emerged as the main driver for Russia's behaviour within the regime. In that context, Russia has also expressed environmental concerns – to convince the partners of the environmental safety of increased energy transport. Environmental argumentation was to some extent present in domestic discussions, but mainly from environmental non-governmental organizations (NGOs) and not those responsible for Russia's negotiations within the regime. And even their concerns were often linked to Russia's image: a civilized country should be able to treat its own sewage. The domestic discussion also noted that the priorities of the Baltic Sea regimes differ from the local environmental concerns most salient to the Russian side. That Russia has not made any significant attempts to advance these priorities within the regime but has agreed to those defined by Western actors serves to demonstrate the importance of non-environmental benefits as the main motivation for Russia's participation.

Clearly, then, Russia's policies have not been primarily motivated by the goal of protecting the environment. There seems to be some variation, in line with the perceived reliability of science: the firmer the scientific basis is considered to be, the more genuine environmental arguments are brought up. In the Baltic Sea case, scientific consensus on the issue of eutrophication has been recognized by the Russian side as well established, and that may have facilitated Russia's closer engagement in the regime. However, an alternative explanation may be the importance of economic interests. The Baltic Sea regime did not entail any significant costs to Russia; so lower-level actors (NGOs) pressing for environmental arguments could be allowed to participate. In the fisheries case, strong local economic interests were involved; in the climate case, the perceived costs were the subject of heated debate in Russia, and future economic burdens seemed likely in any case.

It is also significant that all three cases provide evidence that environmental arguments are seen as a starting point for negotiations on the benefits expected by Russia. Western environmental argumentation is well known and has often been followed by Russia when seeking or justifying benefits, especially related to financial and foreign policy. In fact, this can introduce some of the environmental concerns discussed in the West to the Russian debate. In some cases, environmental protection measures have been launched precisely because of the financial resources available from Western sources. Even though the starting point for this Russian approach may appear somewhat questionable, the outcome can be additional environmental benefits.

However, our starting point is to assume that 'environmental' refers to concern about protecting the environment from damages caused by the activities of our societies *per se*. But is this approach to 'environmental' encounters functional, since it fails to recognize alternative, and potentially relevant, approaches? In order to accommodate the Russian tradition, should an argument be treated as 'environmental' even though it does not have the goal of preventing environmental damage?

The precautionary principle seems alien to the Russian debate, where the role of scientific proof is decisive in domestic decision-making. This flies in the face of the Western belief that action should be taken even before there is full scientific certainty of an environmental problem. The Russian understanding of the environment sees it more as a resource base than as something valuable and worth protecting in its own right. The health impacts suffered by human beings tend to serve an indicator that justifies labelling a problem as 'environmental' in Western terms, that is worth action.

The experience of impacts is also relevant here: it was the emphasis on local wastewater problems (and not actual eutrophication) in the case of the Baltic Sea, and the (im)permanence of the Barents Sea fishing stock that brought the necessity of protection home to many actors – also Russian ones. However, the impacts of climate change are both geographically and temporally unclear and undefined. This makes it very difficult to justify costly (or indeed any) domestic action aimed at mitigating climate change. As a result, other policy goals tend to drive any activities aimed at reducing greenhouse gas emissions.

Here we come to the differences in rhetorical approaches between Russia and the West. From a semantic viewpoint, the Russian concept of 'ecological' seems to be understood more in terms of the natural sciences than its Western counterpart, 'environmental', which is defined more through the social sciences, including political science. With climate issues, 'ecological' can be interpreted to refer to the absolute quantitative outcome of policy measures in the ecosystem. Examples here include the total impact of the Kyoto regime on the concentration of greenhouse gases in the atmosphere, and the share of Russia's forests of the global total. The Western 'environmental' approach – with its politically agreed principles and concepts that lead to the precautionary principle that allows a focus on action to prevent environmental damage regardless of full scientific certainty, or that emphasize the importance of getting started even without sufficient participation to make a physical difference in the atmosphere – appears alien in terms of the Russian discourses.

But does the Russian 'ecological' contain an assumption of environmental concern similar to the Western logic of 'environmental', which boils down to the precautionary principle? This does not seem to be the case. Quite the opposite: Russia approves of the Baltic Sea Action Plan because it is based on ecological facts (ecosystem management approach) without any politics involved. This is one reason why Russia appreciates the Helsinki Commission (HELCOM) – less politics, more ecology. As a result, environmental regimes driven by the precautionary principle may often appear unfounded and thus naïve to a Russian audience. This can also lead Russian actors to abuse the financial flows available for environmental protection purposes if the entire justification for such action seems to lack a rational basis, for instance in direct short-term costs or health impacts on the local population.

Further, it seems easy for Russian actors to point at discrepancies in Western argumentation – when ignoring their starting point as political agreements rather than facts of natural science. Identifying any mistake or suspicious detail, however minor, in the Western analysis may be seen as enough to disqualify the whole Western understanding of the issue. As the scientific uncertainty on climate change continues, and the Kyoto regime cannot have any significant impact on atmospheric concentrations of greenhouse gases, it seems logical to explain the continued Western political support to the Protocol as being motivated by interests of other than environmental origin. The Russian logic then leads to the question of what the 'real' interests behind this support are. And that shows that it is equally difficult for the Russian actors to step out of their discourses as it is to their Western counterparts.

Thus, taking into account the Russian interpretations of the environment itself and the rhetorical approaches related to it, caution should be exercised when outlining environmental goals of international regimes in Western terms. They may appear as something completely different to the Russian side. This could help to explain why Russia's international-level statements may sometimes seem 'weird'. Instead of judging them from the Western viewpoint, it may make more sense to seek a better understanding of the underlying premises. This is not to suggest that genuine environmental concerns can always be identified behind the Russian rhetoric – but it could contribute to establishing environmental goals that are more realistic in terms of their outcomes from the perspective of the environmental regime in question and more understandable to all participants. But in this sense, also the Russian encounter should be seen as 'environmental': a better understanding of its premises can contribute to improving the state of the environment under international regimes.

Having said all this about Russia, to be fair, we should also take a look at the Western approach to the precautionary principle in terms of its practical contributions to protecting the environment. How much are these two issues linked, and how are they linked? Perhaps we in the West embrace the principle at the high political level, but, when it comes to the actual policy choices, similar dynamics apply as in Russia? Do the related benefits, and not the actual environmental concerns, serve to incentivize and drive policies in the West as well? They certainly play a role. Indeed, it could be claimed that the precautionary principle has more a facilitating role in the policy process than actually driving it. Western governments do push for international negotiation processes on the basis of the precautionary principle, that is environmental concerns. This is likely to be a response to the public pressure related to democracy and voting. However, rejections of international level commitments by powerful parties – the US not least – tell a somewhat different story. And this is not a story that unconditionally supports the strength of genuine concerns of the damage inflicted by the activities of our societies on the environment as the main driving force of policy action. In many cases also the West has been motivated by foreign policy goals, even if the environmental worry was genuine. The early history of the Baltic Sea protection regime is a good example of this. Moreover, the concept of the precautionary principle continues to evolve. The EU now considers that the principle has achieved customary status, but that is rather an exception than the rule (Sands et al. 2012, p. 228).

Therefore, we should also give consideration to the Russian criticism of the motivations of the West, even though parts of it are clearly unfounded, driven by geopolitical interests and beliefs. If rhetoric is the main level where environmental concern appears in Russia's policy, the same element can also be identified, albeit perhaps to a lesser extent, in the West. Especially the US and Japan have been seen as regarding precaution as a threat to free markets and technological innovation, and thus trying to soften the principle in international negotiations. The difference between Russia and the West, mainly the EU, may be interpreted as that between strong and weak sustainability position of the precautionary principle: the former allowing the costs of intervention outweigh the obvious benefits, whereas the latter does not allow accepting excessive costs, and adopts a 'wait and see' attitude instead (O'Riordan and Cameron 1994, pp. 20–1). Another explanatory factor behind the differences in the results of environmental policies between the West and Russia may be found in their systems of implementation. In the West, the linkage between adopted policies and their implementation tends to be more straightforward than in Russia, where the weakness of the legal system and its support structures often leave policies adopted, but unimplemented.

Finally, what we can learn from the cases presented here, as regards negotiating with Russia on environmental regimes? As we have covered only three regimes, not all the lessons can be generalized further, and the context of each case must always be taken into account. However, we can sum up some hints of elements that negotiators may encounter.

From our cases, it seems that negotiation partners should not expect environmental concerns to drive Russian policy. Quite the opposite: environmentally based argumentation is more likely to 'mirror' the rhetoric of the negotiation partners in order to promote some other interests, especially those related to foreign policy, national image or economic benefits. Further, for the same reason, it tends to be out of the question for Russia to agree to costly commitments to solve environmental problems; further, 'compensation' in return for supporting an environmental regime that seems important to the other participants is seen as a legitimate request.

Russia sees scientific certainty as a necessary condition for costly domestic environmental measures. That said, participation in regimes where Russia does not consider this condition to be fulfilled is quite possible if commitments are expected to require little domestic action, and some side benefits are available. The concept of fairness tends to be detached from environmental concerns as such: it often ignores environmental impacts as a factor and disregards the 'polluter pays' principle.

Geopolitics and foreign policy interests drive top-level decision-making.

Lower-level stakeholders or their interests are seldom relevant in this process. Influencing Russian policy is extremely difficult for foreign and domestic actors alike, at least beyond introducing ideas into the Russian debate through collaboration with lower-level actors. Such ideas can then be randomly picked up by the executive level if they happen to support the right goals.

References

Aasjord, B. and G. Hønneland (2008), 'Hvem kan telle "den fisk under vann"? Kunnskapsstrid i russisk havforskning', *Nordisk Østforum*, **22**, 289–312.

Aksenova, O. (2006), 'Sotsial'no-ekologicheskie Posledstviia Politicheskogo Reformirovaniia: Ot Tsentralizatsii k Lokalizatsii Ekologicheskoi Politiki Rossii', in N.M. Drobizhev (ed.), *Rossiia Reformiruiushchaiasia: Ezhegodnik – 2005*, Moscow: Institut Sotsiologii RAN.

Andersen M. (2002), 'Ecological modernization or subversion? The effect of Europeanization on Estern Europe', *American Behavioral Scientist*, **45** (9), 1394–416.

Andonova, L. and A. Alexieva (2012), 'Continuity and change in Russia's climate negotiations position and strategy', *Climate Policy* **12**, 614–29.

Andresen, S., E.L. Boasson and G. Hønneland (2012), 'An international environmental policy takes place', in S. Andresen, E.L. Boasson and G. Hønneland (eds), *International Environmental Agreements: An Introduction*, London: Routledge.

Anikin, B.A. (2002), 'Predislovie', in B.A. Anikin (ed.), *Natsionalnaya Ideya Rossii*, Moscow: Dashkov i K°, pp. 4–7.

Århus, T.V. (2012), *Maritim mistru og petroleumspartnarskap: Ein diskursanalyse av russiske reaksjonar på norsk nordområdepolitikk* [*Maritime Suspicion and Petroleum Partnership: a discourse analysis of Russian reactions to Norwegian High North policy*], Master's thesis in European and American Studies – Russian Studies, Oslo: University of Oslo.

Artioli Y., J. Friedrich, A.J. Gilbert, A. McQuatters-Gollop, L.D. Mee, J.E. Vermaat, et al. (2008), 'Nutrient budgets for European seas: a measure of the effectiveness of nutrient reduction policies', *Marine Pollution Bulletin*, **56**, 1609–17. DOI: 10.1016/j.marpolbul.2008.05.027.

Auer, M. and E. Nilenders (2001), 'Verifying environmental cleanup: lessons from the Baltic Sea Joint Comprehensive Environmental Action Programme', *Environmental Planning C*, **19** (6), 881–901.

Averre, D. (2008), 'Russian foreign policy and the global political environment', *Problems of Post-Communism*, **55** (5), pp. 28–39.

Baburin, S. and S. Nebrenchin (2009), *Krizis: Rossiia spaset mir?* Moscow: Astrel.

Barentsnova (2010), *Over-optimistic Shale Gas Bonanza*, available at http://barentsnova.com/node/697 (accessed 26 September 2011).

Barkdull, J. and P.G. Harris (2002), 'Environmental change and foreign policy: a survey of theory', *Global Environmental Politics*, **2** (2), 63–91.

Bartelson, J. (1995), *A Genealogy of Sovereignty*, Cambridge, UK: Cambridge University Press.

Barth, F. (1993), *Balinese Worlds*, Chicago, IL: University of Chicago Press.

Berenboym, B.I., V.A. Borovkov, V.I. Vinnichenko, E.N. Gavrilov, K.V. Drevetnyak, Yu.A. Kovalev, Yu.M. Lepesevich, E.A. Shamray and M.S. Shevelev (2007), 'Chto takoe sinopticheskiy monitoring treski v Barentsevom more?', *Rybnye resursy*, **4**, 24–9.

Borisov, V.M., S.I. Boychuk, G.P. Vanyushin, A.D. Gomonor, D.N. Klyutshkov, B.N. Kotenev, G.G. Krylov and B.M. Shatokhin (2006), *Sinopticheskiy monitoring zapasov treski v Barentsevom more v 2005 g. na osnove ispol'zovaniya sovremennykh issledovatel'skikh tekhnologiy izucheniya bioresursov*, Moscow: VNIRO Publishing.

BP (2012), BP Statistical Review of World Energy, June 2012, available at www.bp.com/assets/bp_internet/globalbp/globalbp_uk_english/ reports_and_publications/statistical_energy_review_2011/STAGING/ local_assets/pdf/statistical_review_of_world_energy_full_report_2012. pdf (accessed 3 December 2012).

Brunila, O.-P. and J. Storgård (2012), 'Oil transportation in the Gulf of Finland in 2020 and 2030', *Publications of the Centre for Maritime Studies A 61*, Turku, Finland: University of Turku, available at http:// urn.fi/URN:ISBN:978–951–29–5141–3.

Brusendorff, A.C. (2006), 'The success of regional solutions in the Baltic', *Sustainable Development Law & Policy*, **7** (1), 62–66.

Budyko, I. and Y. Izrael (eds) (1987), *Antropogennie izmenenie klimata*, Moscow: Gidrometeoizdat.

Chatham House (2011), *REP Seminar Summary: Soft Power. The Means and Ends of Russian Influence*, 31 March, London: Chatham House.

Darst, R. (2001), *Smokestack Diplomacy: Cooperation and Conflict in East–West Environmental Politics*, Cambridge, MA: The MIT Press.

Davies, B. and R. Harré (1990), 'Positioning: the discursive production of selves', *Journal for the Theory of Social Behaviour*, **20**, 43–63.

Dryzek, J. S. (1997), *The Politics of the Earth: Environmental Discourses*, New York: Oxford University Press.

Food and Agriculture Organization (FAO) (2010), *Global Forest Resources Assessment*, main report. FAO Forestry Paper 163, Rome: FAO.

FAO (2012), *Fish, Crustaceans, Molluscs, etc. – World Capture Production,* available at ftp://ftp.fao.org/fi/stat/summary/a1a.pdf (accessed 6 December 2012).

Feldman, D.L. and I. Blokov (2012), *The Politics of Environmental Policy in Russia*, Cheltenham, UK and Northampton, MA, USA: Edward Elgar Publishing.

Foucault, M. (1972), *The Archaeology of Knowledge*, London: Routledge.

Funke, O. (2005), 'Russian environmental security issues: competing frameworks for the future', *International Journal of Environmental Technology Management* **5** (2–3), 246–75.

Glinski, V.D. (2000), *The Essence of Putinism: The Strengthening of the Privatized State*, Ponars Policy Memo 147, Washington, DC: IMEMO.

Glushenkova, H. (1999), 'Environmental administrative change in Russia in the 1990s', *Environmental Politics* **8** (2), 157–64.

Gritsenko, D. (2013), 'The Russian dimension of Baltic maritime governance', *Journal of Baltic Studies* (iFirst), 1–25.

Gupta, J. (2006), 'Environmental multilateralism under challenge?', in E. Newman, R. Thakur and J. Tirmann (eds), *Multilateralism under Challenge? Power, International Order, and Structural Change*, Tokyo: United Nations University Press, pp. 289–307.

Gutner, T.L. (2002), *Banking on the Environment*, Cambridge, MA: The MIT Press.

Haas, P.M. (1993), 'Protecting the Baltic and North Seas', in P.M. Haas, R.O. Keohane and M.A. Levy (eds), *Institutions for the Earth*, Cambridge, MA: The MIT Press.

Hahn, G. (2005), 'Reforming the Federation', in S. White, Z. Gitelman and R. Sakwa (eds), *Developments in Russian Politics 6*, Durham, NC: Duke University Press, pp. 148–67.

Hajer, M.A. (1995), *The Politics of Environmental Discourse: Ecological Modernization and the Policy Process*, Guildford: Oxford University Press.

Hajer, M.A. (1996), 'Ecological modernisation as cultural politics', in S. Lash, B. Szerszynski and B. Wynne (eds), *Risk, Environment and Modernity: Towards a New Ecology*, London: Sage, pp. 246–68.

Hänninen, S. and J. Rytkönen (2004), 'Oil transportation and terminal development in the Gulf of Finland'. *VTT Publications 547*. Espoo, Finland: VTT Technical Research Centre of Finland, available at www.vtt.fi/inf/pdf/publications/2004/P547.pdf.

Helsinki Commission (HELCOM) (1980), 'Assessment of the effects of pollution on the natural resources of the Baltic Sea', *Baltic Sea Environment Proceedings* No. 5A.

HELCOM (1987), 'First periodic assessment of the state of the marine

146 Russia and the politics of international environmental regimes

environment of the Baltic Sea area, 1980–1985, general conclusions', *Baltic Sea Environment Proceedings* No. 17A.

HELCOM (1988), 'Declaration on the protection of the marine environment of the Baltic Sea area, adopted on 15 February 1988 in Helsinki by the ministers responsible for the environmental protection in the Baltic Sea states', available at www.helcom.fi/stc/files/MinisterialDeclarations/ MinDecl1988.pdf (accessed 20 March 2011).

HELCOM (1989), *Convention on the Protection of the Marine Environment of the Baltic Sea Area, 1974*, Helsinki: Helsinki Commission.

HELCOM (1993), *Convention on the Protection of the Marine Environment of the Baltic Sea Area, 1974 (Helsinki Convention)*, available at www.helcom.fi/stc/files/Convention/convention1974.pdf (accessed 9 December 2013).

HELCOM (1996), 'Third periodic assessment of the state of the marine environment of the Baltic Sea area, 1989–1993, Executive Summary', *Baltic Sea Environment Proceedings* No. 64A.

HELCOM (2004a), *30 Years of Protecting the Baltic Sea. HELCOM 1974–2004*, Helsinki: Helsinki Commission.

HELCOM (2004b), *The Fourth Baltic Sea Pollution Load Compilation, Baltic Sea Environment Proceedings 93*, Hensinki: Helsinki Commission, also available at www.helcom.fi/Lists/Publications/BSEP93.pdf.

HELCOM (2007), 'HELCOM Baltic Sea action plan. HELCOM ministerial meeting Krakow, Poland, 15 November 2007', available at www. helcom.fi/stc/files/BSAP/BSAP_Final.pdf (accessed 4 May 2011).

HELCOM (2009), 'Eutrophication in the Baltic Sea. An integrated thematic assessment of the effects of nutrient enrichment in the Baltic Sea region', *Baltic Sea Environment Proceedings* No. 115B.

HELCOM (2013a), *Baltic Sea Action Plan: National follow-up*, available at www.helcom.fi/baltic-sea-action-plan/national-follow-up/ (accessed 5 December 2013).

HELCOM (2013b), *Baltic Sea Action Plan: Nutrient reduction scheme targets*, available at www.helcom.fi/baltic-sea-action-plan/nutrient-reduction-scheme/targets/ (accessed 5 December 2013).

Helle, I. and S. Kuikka (2010), Itämeren öljykuljetusten riskipeli, in S. Bäck, M. Ollikainen, E. Bonsdorff, A. Eriksson, E. Hallanaro, S. Kuikka, M. Viitasalo and M. Walls (eds), *Itämeren tulevaisuus*, Helsinki: Gaudeamus.

Hellman, J., G. Jones and D. Kaufmann (2000), *Seize the State, Seize the Day: State Capture, Corruption and Influence in Transition*, World Bank Policy Research Working Paper No. 2444, Washington, DC: World Bank.

Henry, L. (2010), *Red to Green: Environmental Activism in Post-Soviet Russia*, Ithaca, NY and London: Cornell University Press.

Henry, L. and V. Douhovnikoff (2008), 'Environmental issues in Russia', *Annual Review of Environmental Resources*, **33**, 437–60.

Henry, L. and L. McIntosh Sundstrom (2012), 'Russia's climate policy: international bargaining and domestic modernization', *Europe-Asia Studies*, **64** (7) (September), 1297–322.

Hiltunen, H. (ed.) (1994), *Finland and Environmental Problems in Russia and Estonia*, Helsinki: Finnish Institute of International Affairs.

Hjorth, R. (ed.) (1996), *Baltic Environmental Cooperation: A Regime in Transition*, Linköping, Sweden: Linköping University.

Höhne, N., S. Wartmann, A. Herold and A. Freibauer (2007), 'The rules for land use, land use change and forestry under the Kyoto Protocol – lessons learned for the future climate negotiations', *Environmental Science & Policy*, **10**, 353–69.

Hønneland, G. (1998), 'Compliance in the fishery protection zone around Svalbard', *Ocean Development and International Law*, **29**, 339–60.

Hønneland, G. (1999), 'Co-operative action between fishermen and inspectors in the Svalbard Zone', *Polar Record*, **35**, 207–14.

Hønneland, G. (2000), *Coercive and Discursive Compliance Mechanisms in the Management of Natural Resources: A Case Study from the Barents Sea Fisheries*, Dordrecht, the Netherlands: Springer.

Hønneland, G. (2003), *Russia and the West: Environmental Co-operation and Conflict*, London and New York: Routledge.

Hønneland, G. (2004), *Russian Fisheries Management: The Precautionary Approach in Theory and Practice*, Leiden, the Netherlands: Martinus Nijhoff.

Hønneland, G. (2006), *Kvotekamp og kyststatssolidaritet: Norsk-russisk fiskeriforvaltning gjennom 30 år*, Bergen, Norway: Fagbokforlaget.

Hønneland, G. (2012), *Making Fishery Agreements Work: Post-Agreement Bargaining in the Barents Sea*, Cheltenham, UK and Northampton, MA, USA: Edward Elgar Publishing.

Hønneland, G. (2014), *Arctic Politics, the Law of the Sea and Russian Identity*, Basingstoke: Palgrave Macmillan.

Hønneland, G. and A.-K. Jørgensen (2003), *Implementing International Environmental Agreements in Russia*, Manchester: Manchester University Press.

Hopf, T. (2002), *Social Construction of International Politics: Identities and Foreign Policies, Moscow 1955 and 1999*, Ithaca, NY: Cornell University Press.

Institut Ekonomicheskogo Analiza (2003), Ekonomicheskie posledstviia vozmozhnoi patifikatsii Rossiiskoi Federatsii Kioskogo Protokola.

Inter-governmental Panel on Climate Change (2007), *Climate Change 2007: The Physical Science Basis, Contribution of Working Group I to the Fourth Assessment Report of the Intergovernmental Panel on Climate Change*, Cambridge and New York: Cambridge University Press.

Jakobsen, T. and V.K. Ozhigin (2011), *The Barents Sea: Ecosystem, Resources, Management. Half a Century of Russian–Norwegian Cooperation*, Trondheim, Norway: Tapir Academic Press.

Jensen, Ø. (2011), 'The Barents Sea: the treaty between Norway and the Russian Federation concerning maritime delimitation and cooperation in the Barents Sea and the Arctic Ocean', *International Journal of Marine and Coastal Law*, **26**, 151–68.

Jørgensen, J.H. and G. Hønneland (2006), 'Implementing global nature protection agreements in Russia', *Journal of International Wildlife Law and Policy*, **9** (1), 33–53.

Jørgensen, K.E. (2010), *International Relations Theory: A New Introduction*, Basingstoke: Palgrave Macmillan.

Karmazinov, F.V. (2010), 'Best practices to improve water quality in the Gulf of Finland as exemplified by Vodokanal of St Petersburg', *Baltic Rim Economies*, **6**, 14.

Kiryushin, P., A. Knizhnikov, K.Kochi, T. Puzanova and S. Uvaro (2013), *Popytnyi neftyanoi gaz v Rossii: "Szhigat nelzia, pererabatyvat!" Analiticheskii doklad ob ekonomicheskih i ekologicheskih izderzhkah czhiganiia popytnogo neftianogo gaza v Rossii*, Moscow: WWF.

Klyuev, N.N. (2002), 'Rossiia na Ekologicheskoi Karte Mira', *Izvestiia Akademii Nauk, Seriia Geograficheskaia*, **6**, 5–16.

Kochtcheeva, L. (2009), *Comparative Environmental Regulation in the United States and Russia: Institutions, Flexible Instruments and Governance*, Albany, NY: State University of New York Press.

Kontratev K., K. Losev, M. Ananicheva and I. Chesnokova (2003), 'Tsena Ekologicheskih Uslug Rossii', *Vestnik Rossiiskoi Adademii Nauk*, **2003** (1), 3–11.

Korotkova, S. (2008), *Geoenvironmental Peculiarity of the Baltic Sea*, author's abstract, Moscow.

Korppoo, A. (2005), 'Russian energy efficiency projects: lessons learnt from activities implemented jointly pilot phase', *Energy Policy*, **33**, 113–26.

Korppoo, A., J. Karas and M. Grubb (eds) (2006), *Russia and the Kyoto Protocol: Opportunities and Challenges*, Brookings: The Royal Institute of International Affairs. Energy, Environment and Development Programme.

Korppoo, A. and A. Moe (2008), 'Russian gas pipeline projects under Track 2: case study on the dominant project type', Climate Strategies Briefing Paper, March, available at www.climatestrategies.org/our-research/category/2.html.

Korppoo, A. and T. Spencer (2009), *The Dead Souls: How to Deal with the Russia Surplus?*, FIIA Briefing Paper 39, 4 September, available at: www.upi-fiia.fi/fi/publication/84/.

Korppoo, A. and T. Spencer (2012), 'Synergies and contradictions between Russia's energy security and emission trends', in L. Anceschi and J. Symons (eds), *Energy Security in the Era of Climate Change: The Asia-Pacific Experience*, Basingstoke: Palgrave Macmillan.

Korppoo, A. and A. Vatansever (2012), *A Climate Vision for Russia: From Rhetoric to Action*, Carnegie Policy Outlook, August 2012, available at http://carnegieendowment.org/files/RussiaClimate.pdf.

Kotilainen, J., M. Tysiachniouk, A. Kuliasova, I. Kuliasov and S. Pchelkina (2008), 'The potential for ecological modernization in the Russian context: scenarios from the forest industry'. *Environmental Politics*, **17** (1) (January), 58–77.

Kotov, V. and E. Nikitina (1996), 'Norilsk Nikel: Russia wrestles with an old polluter', *Environment*, **38** (9), 6–37.

Krasner, S.D. (1978), *Defending the National Interest: Raw Materials Investments and US Foreign Policy*, Princeton, NJ: Princeton University Press.

Kuchins, A.C. and I.A. Zevelev (2012), Russian foreign policy: continuity in change, *The Washington Quarterly*, **35** (1), 147–61.

Kuik, O., J. Aerts, F. Berkhout, F. Biermann, J. Bruggink, J. Gupta and R.S.J. Tol (2008), 'Post-2012 climate policy dilemmas: a review of proposals', *Climate Policy*, **8**, 317–36.

Kulyasova, A.A. and I.P. Kulyasov (2002), 'Reorganisation of environmental administration', in J. Kotilainen and J. Kortelainen (eds), *Environmental Transformations in the Russian Forest Industry: Key Actors and Local Development*, Joensuu, Finland: Joensuu University Press, pp. 72–82.

Litfin, K. (1994), *Ozone Discourses: Science and Politics in International Environmental Cooperation*, New York: Columbia University Press.

Makarychev, A. and V. Morozov (2011), Multilateralism, multipolarity and beyond: a menu of Russia's foreign policy strategies, *Global Governance* **1**, 353–73.

Ministerstvo Prirodnyh Resursov i Ekologii Rossiiskoi Federatsii (2010), *Gosudarstvennyi doklad 'O sostaianii i ob ohrane okruzhaiushchei sredy v Rossiiskoi Federatsii v 2009 godu*, available at www.mnr.gov.ru/regula-tory/detail.php?ID=98694 (accessed 2 October 2012).

Mol, A.P.J. (2009), 'Environmental deinstitutionalization in Russia', *Journal of Environmental Policy and Planning*, **11** (3) (August), 223–41.

Morozov, V. (2008), 'Sovereignty and democracy in contemporary Russia: a modern subject faces the post-modern world', *Journal of International Relations and Development*, **11**, 152–80. (doi:10.1057/jird.2008.6)

Nechiporuk, D. and M. Nozhenko (2010), The problems of the protection of the Baltic Sea in the regions of the Russian Federation: The example of the Kaliningrad region, *Baltic Region*, **2** (4), 108–15.

Nechiporuk, D., M. Nozhenko and E. Belokurova (2011), 'Russia – a special actor in Baltic Sea environmental governance', in M. Pihlajamäki and N. Tynkkynen (eds), *Governing the Blue-green Baltic Sea. Societal Challenges of Marine Eutrophication Prevention*, Helsinki: Finnish Institute of International Affairs, pp. 44–54.

Neumann, I.B. (1996), *Russia and the Idea of Europe: A Study in Identity and International Relations*, London: Routledge.

Neumann, I.B. (2001), *Mening, Materialitet, Makt: En Innføring i Diskursanalyse*, Bergen, Norway: Fagbokforlaget.

Nye, J. (2004), *Soft Power: The Means to Success in World Politics*, New York: Public Affairs.

Nygren, B. (2008), *The Rebuilding of Greater Russia: Putin's Foreign Policy towards the CIS*, Abingdon and New York: Routledge.

Nysten-Haarala, S. (2000), *Development of Constitutionalism and Federalism in Russia*, IIASA Interim Report IR-00–042, Laxenburg, Austria: International Institute for Applied Systems Analysis.

Organisation for Economic Co-operation and Development (OECD) (2004), *Reform of Pollution Charges in the Russian Federation: Assessment of Progress and Opportunities and Constraints for Further Improvement*, ENV/EPOC/EAP/POL(2004)1, Paris: OECD.

OECD (2006), *Environmental Policy and Regulation in Russia: The Implementation Challenge*, Paris: OECD.

Oldberg, I. (2012), 'Soft security in the Baltic Sea region. Russian interests in the Council of Baltic Sea States', *Occasional UIpapers No.12*, Stockholm: The Swedish Institute of International Affairs.

Oldfield, J. (2001), 'Russia, systemic transformation and the concept of sustainable development', *Environmental Politics*, **10** (3), 94–110.

Oldfield, J. (2005), *Russian Nature: Exploring the Environmental Consequences of Societal Change*, Aldershot: Ashgate.

Oldfield, J., A. Kouzmina and D. Shaw (2003), 'Russia's involvement in the international environmental process: a research report', *Eurasian Geography and Economics*, **44** (2), 157–68.

Oldfield, J. and D. Shaw (2002), 'Revisiting sustainable development: Russian cultural and scientific traditions and the concept of sustainable development', *Area*, **34** (4), 391–400.

Olimpieva, I. (2010), 'The changing contours of corruption in Russia: informal intermediaries in state–business relations', *Journal of Economics and Business*, **13** (2), 61–82.

Omelyanchuk, O. (2001), *Explaining State Capture and State Capture*

Modes: The Cases of Russia and Ukraine, Budapest: Central European University, Department of International Relations and European Studies.

O'Riordan, T. and J. Cameron (1994), *Interpreting the Precautionary Principle*, Abington: Earthscan.

Ostergren, D. and P. Jacques (2002), 'A political economy of Russian nature conservation policy: why scientists have taken a back seat', *Global Environmental Politics*, **2** (4), 102–24.

Pedersen, T. (2008), 'The constrained politics of the Svalbard offshore area', *Marine Policy*, **32**, 913–19.

Pedersen, T. (2009), 'Norway's rule on Svalbard: tightening the grip on the Arctic islands', *Polar Record*, **45**, 147–52.

Pihlajamäki, M. and N. Tynkkynen (2011a), 'The challenge of bridging science and policy in the Baltic Sea eutrophication governance in Finland: the perspective of science', *AMBIO: A Journal of the Human Environment*, **40** (2), 191–9.

Pihlajamäki, M. and N. Tynkkynen (eds) (2011b), *Governing the Blue-green Baltic Sea. Societal Challenges of Marine Eutrophication Prevention*, FIIA Report 31, Helsinki: The Finnish Institute of International Affairs.

Pihlajamäki, M. and N. Tynkkynen (2011c), 'Introduction', in M. Pihlajamäki and N. Tynkkynen (eds), *Governing the Blue-green Baltic Sea. Societal Challenges of Marine Eutrophication Prevention*, FIIA Report 31, Helsinki: The Finnish Institute of International Affairs, pp. 11–20.

Pouliot, V. (2007), '"Sobjectivism": toward a constructivist methodology', *International Studies Quarterly*, **51** (2), 359–84.

Prezident Rossii (2012), 'Zasedanie prezidiuma Gossoveta po voprosam ekologicheskoi bezopasnosti', available at www.kremlin.ru/news/11519 (accessed 20 November 2012).

Pryde, P.R. (1995), *Environmental Resources and Constraints in the Former Soviet Republics*, Boulder, CO: Westview.

Putnam, R.D. (1988), 'Diplomacy and domestic politics: the logic of two-level games', *International Organization*, **42** (3), 427–60.

Räsänen, T. and S. Laakkonen (2008), 'Institutionalization of an international environmental policy regime: the Helsinki Convention, Finland and the Cold War', in M. Joas, D. Jahn and K. Kern (eds), *Governing the Common Sea: Environmental Policies in the Baltic Sea Region*, London: Earthscan, pp. 43–59.

Roginko, A. (1998), 'Domestic implementation of the Baltic Sea pollution commitments in Russia and the Baltic States', in D.G. Victor, K. Raustiala and E.B. Skolnikoff (eds), *The Implementation and*

Effectiveness of International Environmental Commitments. Theory and Practice, Cambridge, MA: The MIT Press, pp. 575–638.

Roginko, S. (2002), 'Evropa i ee "zelenie" interesi', *Ekspert*, **10**, 11 March.

Rosenau, J. (1969), *Linkage Politics: Essays on the Convergence of National and International Systems*, New York: Free Press.

Røttingen, I., H. Gjøsæter and B.H. Sunnset (2007), 'Norsk-russisk forskersamarbeid 50 år', *Havforskningsnytt*, **16**, Bergen, Norway: Institute of Marine Research.

Rytövuori, H. (1980), 'Structures of détente and ecological interdependence: cooperation in the Baltic Sea area for the protection of the marine environment and living resources', *Cooperation and Conflict: Nordic Journal of International Politics*, **15**, 85–102.

Saari, S. (2014), 'Russia's post-orange revolution strategies to increase its influence in former Soviet republics: public diplomacy *po russkii*', *Europe-Asia Studies*, **66**, (1), 50–66.

Sands, P., J. Peel, A. Fabra and R. MacKenzie (2012), *Principles of Environmental Law*, Cambridge: Cambridge University Press.

Serebryakov, V. and P. Solemdal (2002), 'Cooperation in marine research between Russia and Norway at the dawn of the 20th century', *ICES Marine Science Symposia*, **215**, 73–86.

Stavins, R.N. (2000), 'Market-based environmental policies', in P.R. Portney and R.N. Stavins (eds), *Public Policies for Environmental Protection*, Washington, DC: Resources for the Future (RFF) Press, pp. 31–76.

Stokke, O.S. (2012), *Disaggregating International Regimes: A New Approach to Evaluation and Comparison*, Cambridge, MA, and London: The MIT Press.

Tokunaga, M. (2010), 'Environmental governance in Russia: the "closed pathway" to ecological modernization', *Environment and Planning A*, **42**, 1686–704.

Trumbull, N.S. (n.d.), 'The Helsinki Convention as system of implementation review and its effectiveness for Russia', unpublished manuscript.

Trumbull, N.S. (2007), 'Pressures on urban water resources in Russia: the case of St Petersburg', *Eurasian Geography and Economics*, **48** (4), 495–506.

Tsygankov, A.P. (2010), *Russia's Foreign Policy: Change and Continuity in National Identity*, Lanham, MD: Rowman & Littlefield.

Tsygankov, A. (2012), 'Assessing cultural and regime-based explanations of Russia's foreign policy. "Authoritarian at heart and expansionist by habit"?', *Europe-Asia Studies*, **64** (4), 695–713.

Tsygankov, A. (2013), 'Moscow's soft power strategy', *Current History*, **112** (756), 259–64.

Tsygankov, A. (2014), 'Contested identity and foreign policy: interpreting Russia's international choices', *International Studies Perspectives*, **15**, 19–35.

Tynkkynen, N. (2006), 'Action frames of environmental organisations of post-Soviet St. Petersburg', *Environmental Politics*, **15** (4), 639–49.

Tynkkynen, N. (2008a), *Constructing the Environmental Regime between Russia and Europe. Conditions for Social Learning*, volume 1301 of Acta Universitatis Tamperensis, Tampere, Finland: Tampere University Press.

Tynkkynen, N. (2008b) 'Environmental cooperation and learning: The St. Petersburg water sector. A manuscript', in N. Tynkkynen, *Constructing the Environmental Regime between Russia and Europe. Conditions for Social Learning*, Volume 1301 of Acta Universitatis Tamperensis, Tampere, Finland: Tampere University Press.

Tynkkynen, N. (2010), 'Russia, a great ecological power in global climate policy? Framing climate change as a policy problem in Russian public discussion', *Environmental Politics*, **19** (2), 179–95.

Tynkkynen, N. (2011), The future of HELCOM: adaptation or abolition? in M. Pihlajamäki and N. Tynkkynen (eds), *Governing the Blue-green Baltic Sea: Societal Challenges of Marine Eutrophication Prevention*, FIIA Reports 31 Helsinki: The Finnish Institute of International Affairs, pp. 21–32.

Tynkkynen, N. (2013), 'The challenge of environmental governance in the network society: the case of the Baltic Sea', *Environmental Policy and Governance*, **23** (6), 395–406. DOI: 10.1002/eet.1621.

United Nations Development Programme (UNDP) (2010), *National Human Development Report in the Russian Federation: Energy Sector and Sustainable Development*, Moscow: UNDP, available at www.undp.ru/documents/180-eng2–01–04.pdf (accessed 20.6.2012).

VanDeveer, S.D. (2004), 'Ordering environments: regions in European international environmental cooperation', in S. Jasanoff and M. Long Martello (eds), *Earthly Politics. Local and Global in Environmental Governance*, Cambridge, MA: The MIT Press.

VanDeveer, S.D. (2011), 'Networked Baltic environmental cooperation', *Journal of Baltic Studies*, **42**, 37–55. DOI: 10.1080/01629778.2011.538516.

Vesitalous (2012), 'Vesiosaamisen vienti' (special issue on the export of Finnish know-how on water management), *Vesitalous*, **53** (1).

Vodokanal (2001), *Final Report of the Corporate Development Support Programme*, St Petersburg, Russia: Vodokanal of St Petersburg.

Vylegzhanin, A.N. and V.K. Zilanov (2007), *Spitsbergen: Legal Regime of*

Adjacent Marine Areas, Utrecht, the Netherlands: Eleven International Publishing.

World Commission on Environment and Development (1987), *Our Common Future: Towards Sustainable Development*, Oxford: Oxford University Press.

Yanitsky, O. (2007), *Ekologicheskaia Kul'tura: Ocherki vzaimodeistviia nauki i Praktiki*, Moscow: Nauka.

Index